In the Shadow

with Jesus

In the Shadow with Jesus

A Look at the High Priestly Prayer of John 17

Larry L. Armstrong

FaithProbe

ISBN 13: 978-0-9823466-1-7
ISBN 10: 0-9823466-1-1

Contents

Preface

My study of Jesus' high priestly prayer began in a seminary course on John's gospel, but it was part of the study of the entire gospel. I remember being impressed by the knowledge that shortly before his crucifixion Jesus prayed for his disciples—and for me and all Christians who'd believe in the apostles' witness. The idea gave me a warm comfort.

After seminary, I picked up H. C. G. Moule's, *The High Priestly Prayer*, reprinted by Baker Book House from the 1907 edition. However, Moule's work began in 1875 as a series of discussion papers shared on Sunday evenings with students at Trinity College, Cambridge, England. I used this classic book in my daily devotions during January 1979, making marginal notes and underlining many thoughts.

I eventually preached a series of sermons on John 17 in one of my pastorates, and now again, I've completed a series of messages on the prayer which are the foundation of this book. For years I've intended to write on John 17 in a meditative style, allowing Jesus' thoughts and mood on his final evening to stimulate my thinking.

Here's what intrigues me about the high priestly prayer. It's the record of the petitions Jesus made to his heavenly Father an hour or so before he was arrested. He spoke aloud, and John pieced together a remembrance of the Lord's final intimate conversation with both God and his disciples. Here's an opportunity to overhear what pressured the Savior's heart as he moved quickly and finally toward the immense sacrifice he was called to make. Surely, what he said publicly at that moment is important for you and me to understand.

After years of reflection, I humbly offer my awareness of what seems to have been in his thoughts. I also suggest ways to apply what concerned him to what concerns us in daily life. My desire is to awaken in you a passion to know what your Lord felt, desired and prayed only an hour or so before his arrest. Understanding this, you'll be better able to complete his will in your conduct and witness.

You're encouraged to read this book and the prayer with an attitude of meditation. Think about Jesus' words over and over. Pray about them. Consider my thoughts about his prayer, and write out your understandings. You may want to gather with Christian friends to read the prayer and discuss its lessons, as Moule did with his Cambridge students.

Give serious devotional effort to this work, and you'll grow in your love for Jesus, the high priest who prayed for you.

Larry Armstrong

Chapter One

In the Shadow with Jesus

Shadows are fearful. As you walk close to them, they take on shapes that don't become clearly discernible. You might decide nothing's there or discover what you most dread. In Psalm 11, an ancient poet spoke about taking refuge in the Lord because he felt like a defenseless bird when hunters "shoot from the shadows" (v. 2). He was apprehensive because the upright in heart have to be wary of those with evil intent. In a forest, shade can be foreboding, black, and if you walk at dusk in a woods full of ravines and hillocks you may not be pleased when clouds pass overhead. You sense how death lurks in the "valley of the shadow."

In John 13-17, gloominess floats over both Jesus and his disciples during their final night together in an upper room of a house in Jerusalem—the shadow of Christ's cross. To understand the high priestly prayer of Jesus in

John 17, which is the goal of this book, you need to be aware of the context given in the four preceding chapters. You have to intrude on the dimness of the upper room. So let's pace around the fearful space and discover in its silhouettes the remarkable lessons Jesus has for those who go into the shadow with him.

The apostle John recorded in his gospel the mind of Jesus as he arrived at the somber banquet. "It was just before the Passover Feast. Jesus knew that the time had come for him to leave this world and go to the Father. Having loved his own who were in the world, he now showed them the full extent of his love" (Jn. 13:1). The cloud was already enveloping Jesus. His departure from both the earth and the disciples lay heavily on him. The joy of returning to the Father was in his heart, but the excitement was tempered by an imminent separation. The work of salvation, for Jesus, was tinged with joy and sorrow from beginning to end. As we read the high priestly prayer, we'll discover over and over the mixed emotions our Lord carried in his heart on the eve of his crucifixion. For Jesus, the shadow went from gray to black, and it became dreary in the upper room.

Usually the thought expressed in John 13:1 is applied to the event that follows in the narrative. "Having loved his own who were in the world," John explained, "he now showed them the full extent of his love." Then Jesus wrapped himself in a towel, washed the disciples' feet and ordered them to serve one another in love—to follow his example. But before telling this story from Christ's last hours, John said something else that added depth to the first verse. He recorded: "The evening meal was being served, and the devil had already prompted Judas Iscariot, son of Simon, to betray Jesus" (Jn. 13:2). The Lord sat at the Passover table and anticipated his reunion with his Father, a return to full intimacy that only a father and son who've been separated for a lifetime can know. Jesus also felt chagrin at leaving Peter, John, Matthew, James, and the others of his band. Yet Judas Iscariot's planned betrayal darkened the evening in Christ's heart. John's narrative hinted at the ecstasy, sadness and distress Jesus endured during his final night. The evening was destined to become sacred in Christian memory, but when it was experienced by the Lord Jesus, the night wrenched his heart.

Judas Iscariot's silhouette dimmed the upper room, and it prepares us to hear the prayer at the close of this intense night. Before Jesus served the disciples as a foot washing slave, we read about a traitor and think about a crushing disloyalty from one who'd been trusted, loved and kept close for years. We're aware that his feet were among those made wet and dried by a divine hand whose touch was so human. The coming treachery of Judas' kiss was put in poignant relief against Jesus' humble stooping, washing, loving. Beneath the table's flickering light, the Savior's devotion stretched forth to stroke two feet that would soon walk angrily from the upper room and carry their owner to priests who were all too willing to become accomplices in the lost disciple's rejection.

We know Jesus thought about Judas as they entered the Jerusalem home where he'd ate with the disciples one last time, because he himself raised the issue of infidelity. He quoted Psalm 41:9 which spoke about one who ate bread with another and lifted his heel against the host. Then he was plain in his statement: "I tell you the truth, one of you is going to betray me" (Jn. 13:21). In stunned confusion, the disciples stared at one another. Peter tried to get another disciple to find out who was meant, and this follower of Christ was shown that the traitor was Judas Iscariot by a revealing action. The gospel writer John commented: "As soon as Judas took the bread, Satan entered into him" (Jn. 13:27a).

What did the bread signify? Was it a convicting action that made Judas all the more ready to betray his Master? Was it intended merely to identify for the disciple who asked the question who was meant prior to the man's identity becoming public knowledge? In Jesus' hand, the bread must have felt like a heavy burden. He knew he gave it to the traitor who'd bring him to apparent ruin. In 1882, Frederick Denison Maurice commented on the giving of the bread:

> ...it has been the belief of all earnest men of all schools that the sop given to Judas was a last love-token, and that the entrance of Satan into him, after it had been received, expresses that last defiance of love, that utter abandonment to the spirit of selfishness, which precedes the commission of the greatest conceivable crime.

Maurice felt that his nineteenth century contemporaries considered the bread (the "sop") to be an expression of love for Judas by Jesus, which the disciple defied and rejected. Having abandoned Christ's expression of love for him, Judas was defeated by selfishness, and so he committed the most heinous crime in history—betrayal of Jesus the Nazarene to enemies. Sin abandoned the Savior's love and accepted satanic destruction.

Meditate on Judas' rejection of Jesus Christ's affection. Could you discard your Master's fondness for you and his passion for your rescue? Would you accept the "sop" and walk away, then return later to kiss the one whom you once believed possessed all the answers for which you searched? I'd guess that most of us wouldn't want to enter into such a shadow, but the truth is quite different. Every one of us, prior to knowing Jesus, and now and then after associating with him, are prone to betray him. Be honest. When did you deceive God's Son, and yourself, regarding loyalty to him? Anyone can betray Jesus.

Only a moment after telling of the bread, John added, "As soon as Judas had taken the bread, he went out. And it was night" (Jn. 13:30). *It was night.* I've always found this short sentence to be a heart-twisting revelation. Judas, a frustrated disciple, went into the shadowy valley, alone and defenseless, determined to complete what he shouldn't have agreed to do. He stopped walking with Jesus and strode out against him as a treacherous warrior would turn in battle to kill his commander and give the victory to the enemy. His unfaithfulness was painted with a nocturnal blackness, the color preferred by predator or marauder. Feel sorry for Judas if you must—and many today do feel remorseful for him—but Judas was still a traitor to one who loved him dearly. He went out from the fellowship of the upper room, and it was night.

In the evening, shadows rise and grow larger than life. Remember walking down the street after dark toward your house as a child? The streetlights made a neighbor's bushes seem bigger than during the day, and your fear elevated with the height of the shrubbery. Was somebody hiding nearby? Would he grab you? Unsure, you walked faster, and soon you ran, glancing over a shoulder, almost racing past your porch and its safety. I think Judas left so quickly after receiving the bread because he was running from his own shadow, fearful, since his plot with the priests had been found out. He ran from Christ's love and from a cross he himself helped to manufacture.

Judas wasn't the only disciple with Jesus in the upper room who was touched by the cross' profile. Pace around the table. Look at Simon Peter. He also experienced the obscurity of this awesome night. Peter watched Jesus scrub the other disciples' feet, and as the Teacher reached him, he was horrified and drew his feet aside. "No, Lord! Not my feet!" But Jesus insisted that the washing was necessary if Simon was to share Christ, that is, to belong to the loving and serving Messiah. The disciple then declared that, in this case, he'd welcome a full bath: "Wash everything, Lord!" Jesus must have snickered at the thought since he teased back. "You don't need a bath, Peter. Washing the feet is enough." Then, I think, Jesus cast a look around the table and said, in effect, "Most of you are clean." I'm sure his gaze went from person to person. Eyes met his and averted themselves in fear that Jesus knew what was in the heart. The eyes are the window of the soul, after all! Jesus, of course, meant Judas

Iscariot. He wasn't among those who'd be faithful, yet Jesus implied that Peter and the other guests in the upper chamber were loyal to him, though they wobbled, too.

Shortly after Judas stepped into the night, Simon Peter stepped into his own version of the crucifying shadow, into an agony he himself would experience as Jesus suffered for human sin. Christ spoke about the Father glorifying him and about the disciples looking for him without success. Peter's usual hastiness prompted him to interrupt the Lord as he started to speak about the disciples' need to love one another. He wanted to return to the subject of Jesus' departure and asked where the Lord was going. His Teacher told him he couldn't follow just yet, although he'd follow in the future. He referred to Simon Peter's later crucifixion, but from the shadows of his own mind, Peter asked, "Lord, why can't I follow you now? I will lay down my life for you" (Jn. 13:37). The Rock believed he was ready to meet death if that was what Jesus intended for the two of them. He revealed his shortsightedness. He still didn't comprehend what Jesus was doing or why.

The Lord answered Peter in words that should have chilled his heart as well as his enthusiasm. "Will you really lay down your life for me?" Jesus asked, implying doubt about Peter's sincerity. "I tell you the truth, before the rooster crows, you will disown me three times!" (Jn. 13:38) This statement must have hit Peter with the force of a stone smacking his nose. Jesus couldn't have sounded more harsh. Peter expressed his readiness to be executed beside the Nazarene, to take a place which, unknown to him, was to be occupied by a criminal in the morning. For the moment, Peter reeled from a verbal pummeling by one whom he loved as much as life itself. Jesus plunged Peter into the darkness of crucifixion and the labor of redemptive suffering. Pain like the pain Jesus felt over Judas' betrayal was now knifing through Simon's soul. If he'd have been less of a man, he'd have cried at that moment, in front of his colleagues, weeping as he was destined to weep later in the night after a rooster crowed and he ran away alone.

Was Christ cruel to a loving heart? No, I don't think so. Jesus was bringing a miss-thinking disciple into the reality of the work being done on the cross the following morning. He thumped on Peter's ego in order to prepare him for the events of both the late night and the next day, as well as weeks and years ahead. On an unsteady Rock, Jesus planned to build his church. Peter had confessed him as the Christ, the Messiah, Son of the living God. But the man possessed so many rough wooden edges that needed to be sanded and smoothed and worked into a durable surface by a master carpenter. Love sometimes speaks words that sound cruel but are life-shaping and maturing. Peter's hurt tonight meant his holiness and usefulness in the future. By standing in a shadow for a while, Simon could become a bright witness for his Master. Jesus wasn't cruel; he was compassionate as he told Peter about his imminent, triple betrayal.

Jesus wasn't insensitive to the anguish he gave Simon and the rest of the disciples. On the heels of his comment about denial, he spoke to all his followers in the upper room. "Do not let your hearts be troubled," he said. "Trust in God; trust also in me" (Jn. 14:1). He continued with the now famous words that are read at funerals, words about many rooms in the Father's house. He was comforting his distressed entourage.

Throughout chapter 13 of John's gospel, Jesus tried to teach them about service out of love, but his teaching was interrupted by clouds crossing over the room. Now he brought up the purpose for his return to heaven. He was going to prepare places for them. I think the Savior's intent was to give the group another example of loving service. His journey to the heavenly Father was an act of compassion for them...also for you and me! To serve his followers was Christ's resolve. He knew what was coming years and centuries ahead, and he wanted to comfort the disciples, who'd need this example of tender persistence while a new era in human history erupted on the next morning.

Twice more friends barge into Jesus' instruction. First, Thomas spoke from the gloominess in his own heart. "Lord, we don't know where you are going, so how can we know the way?" (Jn. 14:5) The answer was the Lord's celebrated statement about being the way, truth and life. Thomas should have known but he was ever the skeptic, the cynic of the group. After the raising of the dead Christ, this same disciple would become known as doubting Thomas because he'd then want to touch the rejuvenated Lord before he believed in the truth of his resurrection. Jesus tried now to impress upon him that finding the way to God the Father required following God the Son. Thomas' doubts would keep him in the dimness of half-faith for a while.

Another silhouette around the table was Philip, who was the next to interrupt Jesus' teaching. He said, "Lord, show us the Father and that will be enough for us" (Jn. 14:8). Christ's patience may have been wearing thinner, because he scolded Philip for spending years with him without recognizing his identity. Why should a faithful disciple ask to be shown the heavenly Father? "Don't you believe that I am in the Father, and that the Father is in me?" (Jn. 14:10) After admonishing Philip, Jesus spoke words that sound as if he were speaking to a Pharisee or someone else who didn't accept him as Messiah. Philip should recognize that Jesus' words were from God, not of his own concoction. Or he should look at Jesus' miracles. These two evidences of his unity with the Father and the Father's unity with him ought to be enough for Philip and the others who witnessed this reprimand.

Jesus started to discipline the others, too. He spoke about the works his followers could do if they had faith in him. They'd do works *greater* than he did! Jesus spoke out of frustration with Thomas, Philip, and the others, but his words were a promise of success in loving service, if they imitated the compassionate ministry he'd performed among them—as he'd perform more dramatically over the next few hours, his last hours. Despite his annoyance, the Lord made a bigger promise: "You may ask me for anything in my name, and I will do it" (Jn. 14:14). *Anything!* The other disciples, who were apparently as slow as Philip to count on Jesus' unity with God, would be able to do more than Jesus himself did. Their success depended on meeting two criteria: faith in his oneness with God and reliance on his help in their ministries.

Shadows loom large in the upper room, don't they? But they extend into your life and mine, too. How strong is your belief that Jesus and the Father are one God—Father and Son—who lead you in the merciful service that characterizes Christian living? What would you dare to ask the Lord to do through you? He promises to do anything you request, provided your activities honor his name. There's no act of loving assistance too great for Christ to accomplish through you if you'll trust and obey. Why do you allow the dark outlines of doubt or partial faith to pull you away from success as a servant of God? You can ask Jesus anything. If you believe and act in his name, he'll grant your request. Perhaps not in the manner you expect or instantaneously, but he will bring about the good you propose to do in his name,

However, do you understand what's required of you? Examine your duty carefully. As he told his friends in the Jerusalem house, Jesus tells you, "If you love me, you will obey what I command" (Jn. 14:15). Obedience is required from you and me as surely as it was enlisted from Philip, Thomas, Simon Peter and the rest. Compliance becomes a watchword throughout the remainder of John 13-16 and into the high priestly prayer. To comply with Christ requires you to abide in him, to draw both your wisdom and your life from the Lord. As you study these chapters, observe how obedience develops and ask yourself how Jesus wants you to apply his lessons in today's world.

Respect for his will, deference to it, and conformity to it draw a thick line between successful discipleship and failure as a follower of the Christ.

In his aggravation with the dark silhouettes around the table, Jesus continued his insistent words, but he altered his approach to the call for his disciples to serve lovingly in his name. Jesus pledged himself to seek for them a second Counselor from the Father—the Holy Spirit.

> "If you love me, you will obey what I command. And I will ask the Father, and he will give you another Counselor to be with you forever—the Spirit of truth. The world cannot accept him, because it neither sees him nor knows him. But you know him, for he lives with you and will be in you. I will not leave you as orphans; I will come to you.
>
> John 14:15-18

He continued and explained that the world—that is, the mass of humanity who don't accept him as Savior and Lord—wouldn't perceive his identity as God's Son. Yet the disciples were to discover, after Jesus' resurrection, the unity they shared with the Father and Son. Their insight into this new relationship resulted from their love and obedience. The Lord encouraged his followers to rely on his guidance and advice. Then he could show himself to them.

Once again, a disciple butted in and disturbed the train of Jesus' teaching. A different follower named Judas, who wasn't from Iscariot, interjected, "But, Lord, why do you intend to show yourself to us and not to the world?" (Jn. 14:22) As I read this section of the gospel, it seems to me that Jesus gave up trying to answer the disciples' questions, because he didn't explain anything to this loyal Judas. The Lord simply continued to talk about love and service in his name, about the Holy Spirit and peace, about not being bothered or fearful. He almost accused those in the upper room of not loving him, otherwise they'd be glad he returned to the Father. He pointed out that the "prince of this world" (Jn. 14:30) was about to arrive. Didn't he mean Satan? Was he speaking about the devil-inspired betrayal soon to be implemented by the fickle Iscariot? Yet Jesus promised that Satan and Judas would fail because he himself was obedient to the Father's will, an example for any of his followers who discerned the truth of what he said.

At this point in John's narrative, a comment made by Jesus causes scholars to think the apostle John used several sources for chapters 13-17. Jesus announced, "Come now; let us leave" (Jn. 14:31c). Yet John narrates no departure. The next words are still from Jesus, and they contain the famous image of the vine and branches, together with a call to "abide in me." Perhaps the scholarly opinion is correct, but the continuation of Jesus' teaching

21

during this sacred night leaves John's readers with an unmistakable impression: Christ pressed forward with his final speech—his last lessons—for the disciples. In John 15 and the first half of John 16, Jesus recapitulated all that he'd been saying since he washed the disciples' feet. The narration feels as if John hoped to show how Jesus persisted with delivering the core of his instructions all over again. He was desperate. He wanted his followers to be prepared for the crucifixion and resurrection, as well as the aftermath of these shattering events. But they were still boarding the ship! They didn't comprehend. The confusion of his followers jeopardized his successful redemption of humanity. Were they ready to take over his mission? Perhaps he wasn't certain they were.

Jesus continued to talk of many subjects: remaining in his love, giving one's life on behalf of friends, calling the disciples his friends, bearing a durable fruit, society's hatred and persecution, and the world's rejection of his witness about the Father. He returned to the Holy Spirit's work of witnessing about him and to the disciples' own testimony for him. Jesus continued into the first half of John 16 without interruption from anyone in the upper room. Then he warned about the disciples' imminent sufferings. At this point, he nodded to their frustration. "Now I am going to him who sent me," he commented, "yet none of you asks me, 'Where are you going?' Because I have said these things, you are filled with grief" (Jn. 16:5-6). He spoke about the Spirit's arrival as a result of his departure from earth. The Spirit would convict the world and counsel the disciples. They'd learn truth from a Counselor, who'd glorify Christ.

Then Jesus uttered a thought that brought another interruption from the room's shadow-covered occupants. He said, "In a little while you will see me no more, and then after a little while you will see me" (Jn. 16:16). Not a new comment, but repeated now with emphasis. This night was a genuine parting of the ways. The full room would become empty without Christ; the band of learners was losing their center point, the fulcrum on which their lives had been balancing for years. Chatter arose around the table. People wondered what Jesus meant by "a little while," by seeing him no more, by his retreat to the Father's presence. The hubbub indicated how little they perceived what Jesus told them. In a lengthy response, Jesus announced a blending of grief and joy that awaited his followers when he left. He reassured them of the Father's willingness to meet their needs during the time of turmoil. They merely had to ask in his name. Jesus also pledged himself to seek the Father's blessing for the church. He bolstered them with another reminder that the Father himself loved Jesus' followers. He concluded by saying, "I came from the Father and entered the world; now I am leaving the world and going back to the Father" (Jn. 16:28). A final disruption in the upper room's dim light. The disciples confessed that Jesus no longer spoke in riddles. They understood him plainly. Yet readers of John's gospel wonder if the followers recognized the truths just spoken. Indeed, Jesus also questioned their newfound knowledge.

> "You believe at last!" Jesus answered. "But a time is coming, and has come, when you will be scattered, each to his own home. You will leave me all alone. Yet I am not alone, for my Father is with me.
>
> John 16:31-32

The Lord almost mocked the disciples: "You believe at last!" This rendering makes his words appear as if Jesus communicated renewed frustration with doltish disciples who thought they had finally measured up to his high expectations.

The *New International Version* contains an alternate translation in a footnote: "Do you now believe?" The question can be interpreted as either a skeptical remark or a serious inquiry. To me, the sentence carries the weight of doubt. Jesus wasn't confident his followers were keeping up with him. He stepped into the cross' shadow with uncertainty about the success of his mission and with little more than faith in the Father to carry him forward. His remarks about the disciples' scattering and the abandonment to his fate support this understanding of Jesus' mood as he turned to God in the high priestly prayer. Christ started his prayer in a despondent mood. His heart broke, his faith was strong, but he worried.

This is the context in which we need to study the high priestly prayer from John 17, and for me it sheds much light on my Lord's sad heart and unclear frame of mind as the crucifixion loomed large. He was afraid his mission might not succeed. The world might not be redeemed!

This hesitant context also reveals the historical reality of Christ's life. He didn't simply come into the world, see its needs and reveal an answer, then conquer sin and despair by divine power. He invaded the territory of the "prince of this world" (Jn. 16:11) and defeated him by his own human sorrow and insecurity. Yes, he had the power of angels at his disposal, but Jesus chose to endure an agony of the human soul while he redeemed the human beings who would believe. Jesus went to the cross as the God-man, but his divine and human heart was shaken and pressed hard. It's little wonder to me that he turned to the Father in prayer at the conclusion of a difficult last night with his people. He spoke aloud, still desiring that the disciples should benefit from his mind's troubled state, but praying from his own erupting emotions and anxiety. The high priest who prayed was seeking to be blessed while being a blessing. Once more we see Jesus, loving servant of both God and humanity, the supreme example of the kind of people you and I were created to be, until we lost fellowship with our Creator because of sin. He was also the exemplar we're called to replicate for others who might yet be redeemed.

I invite you to walk into the shadow with Jesus. He has much more to teach us.

Chapter Two

What Jesus Wanted for Himself

IN HIS EPIC POEM, *Sohrab and Rustrum,* Matthew Arnold has the dying Sohrab say to an enemy:

> Man, who art thou who dost deny my words?
> Truth sits upon the lips of dying men,
> And falsehood, while I lived, was far from mine.
>
> *Lines* 655-657

Though a literary character, his words express a common opinion. A dying person tells no lies.

The last words a person speaks, when he knows his end draws near, are important words. They sum up the life lived, the person's character and dreams. When your days on earth are finished, how do you hope family and friends will honor your memory? Consider your days and deeds well when you approach their completion. What do you want to leave behind in people's memories?

Your last words are expected to be the best you'll ever utter. They'll be what people remember about you after you're gone. Many daughters and sons recall a parent's advice even decades after the funeral's sad day. If they sat nearby when the death occurred, they hug the memory of a final shared conversation. When no final words passed between parent and child, friend and friend, the living one often wishes she'd said something that now lingers unspoken and haunting.

Some of us wonder, along with Ryan Adams, "Can you still have any famous last words if you're somebody nobody knows?" I've never met anybody whom nobody knew! Even the loneliest person in a nursing home who has no living relatives and whose friends have forgotten he's still alive has the folks who take care of him and those who live with him. On my countless trips into such places, I've seen how a home's staff have hearts that break when somebody in their charge dies. Their friends in the home also express sorrow. The final things you say may never be famous, but they may still linger in the thoughts of others.

Jesus of Nazareth wasn't different from you and me in this respect. When he finished his last evening with the disciples in the upper room, having washed their feet and instituted a sacrament, he knew his work was completed.

He wanted to leave parting thoughts in their minds. So he lifted his eyes to heaven and prayed aloud in words the disciples never forgot, words the apostle John recorded. In his prayer, we notice what the Lord wanted as he approached the cross. *Jesus wanted to see his work and his Father honored.* Here lies his verbal legacy to his beloved followers. We do well to consider his wish.

Meditation on Christ's parting thoughts will enhance who you are, what you do, where you go, and what you say among people who share your present days, and perhaps your final ones. His thoughts will help you to assess the legacy you'll leave behind.

Jesus' Hour

Your Lord knew the auspicious moment had come. His *hour* had arrived. He was about to die because of your sin. So Jesus prayed, "Father, the time has come. Glorify your Son, that your Son may glorify you" (Jn. 17:1*b*). The Bible in the *New International Version* uses the word "time," but the Greek word is "hour." Jesus said his *hour* had come. He knew the auspicious moment had arisen.

Jesus used the same word, *hour*, when he spoke to his mother at the wedding in Cana. She wanted him to do something because the wine was running out. What she expected isn't spelled out, but she apparently understood that Jesus could work some kind of miracle. He chose to turn water into wine, but before he performed the first public sign of his deity, the Gospel of John reported what the Lord said to Mary. "Dear woman, why do you involve me?" Jesus replied. "My time [*my hour*] has not yet come" (Jn. 2:4).

On another occasion, Jesus defended his healings on the Sabbath. As enemies already plotted to kill him, he said, "I tell you the truth, a time is coming and has now come when the dead will hear the voice of the Son of God and those who hear will live" (Jn. 5:25). Once again the word *time* is *hour* in the Greek. In the middle years of his ministry, Jesus perceived that his work meant salvation for human beings. The dead he referred to may have been people who were literally in their graves, or the reference might be symbolic language, meaning living people who were dead in sin. Either way, Jesus told opponents that his mission on earth was to bring life. His healings on the Lord's day were permissible because he rescued people in severe need. In him, an auspicious age had arrived within humanity's realm. His actions on the Sabbath were in line with God's will. They declared the arrival of the hour of deliverance.

New life was a gift of God's grace, but his opponents dismissed it. As he warned them, "Do not be amazed at this, for a time is coming when all who are in their graves will hear his voice and come out—those who have done good will rise to live, and those who have done evil will rise to be condemned" (Jn. 5:28-29). Again, the word *time* is *hour*.

Throughout his life, Jesus had a goal which he called his *hour*, the moment for which he came into the world. The goal of Jesus' mission was to reveal God the Father and to die for humanity's sins. When he accomplished the two related goals, he'd reach his *hour*, his appointed time. With the disciples the last night in the upper room, Jesus announced that his destiny had arrived. He was about to die then rise again. The Father was revealed, and sinners were about to be redeemed. In other words, on the night of the Gethsemane betrayal, your Lord knew the auspicious moment was upon him.

At this awesome juncture, at his "moment in time," Jesus asked one thing of his Father before he went to the Mount of Olives to meet up with Judas Iscariot. He asked, "Glorify your Son, that your Son may glorify you" (Jn. 17:1*b*).

What's the glory Jesus was concerned about?

In the Old Testament, God's glory was sometimes shown as a bright light within a cloud. At the tabernacle in the wilderness, a dazzling cloud revealed the divine presence after the tent was erected. The Book of Exodus closes with an explanation of what happened:

> Then the cloud covered the Tent of Meeting, and the glory of the Lord filled the tabernacle. Moses could not enter the Tent of Meeting because the cloud had settled upon it, and the glory of the Lord filled the tabernacle.
>
> In all the travels of the Israelites, whenever the cloud lifted from above the tabernacle, they would set out; but if the cloud did not lift, they did not set out—until the day it lifted. So the cloud of the Lord was over the tabernacle by day, and fire was in the cloud by night, in the sight of all the house of Israel during all their travels.
>
> Exodus 40:34-35

The glorious cloud above the tabernacle signaled where God could be found among the wandering Israelites. The divine glory was meant to comfort, caution, and conduct the newly gathered people during their journey to the promised land. God was with his people.

In the New Testament, on the mountain where Jesus was transfigured beside Moses and Elijah, his clothing shone more brightly than any earthly textile worker could produce, and a brilliant light enveloped the trio of holy men. Then a cloud covered the company and God's voice spoke from the cloud. Divine glory, when present to human sight, is a majestic, splendorous light, but the most significant point about the glory is the *presence* of God. When heavenly light shines, you know God is with you. Jesus asked that God's presence be made known to humanity when he died and rose again. Your Lord had one dying wish that embraced all his other desires. He wanted people to see God in his dying. Jesus wanted his work and his Father honored.

Thinking about the end of your life isn't a happy pastime for people. We wish to live forever and not have to face the final curtain. As it closes, terror comes upon many, especially those who have no hope for life beyond the present visible horizon. Henry Fielding wrote in 1751, "It hath been often said, that it is not death, but dying which is terrible" (*Amelia*, III.4).

As a Christian, you should prepare for your exiting speech, or your story of faith in Christ may not move forward. The lead character in a theatrical play is often given a memorable sentence to utter before going off stage. What will you tell those around the room? What do you want them to remember?

Your daily conduct, as well, should speak in case your voice is too feeble at the end. What will the people close to you remember? A kindness? Patience? Joy? Your firm reliance on Jesus Christ? Your legacy is important, and putting off all thought about it may be dangerous. You'll allow opportunities for building a godly reputation to shrink or evaporate. Suddenly, your hour will be upon you. What'll you say? Why? How? What will be your soul's legacy for all its travail in this world? Think! Think now before the hour strikes!

Christ Jesus thought in advance and knew what to tell the disciples, but he told them via an audible prayer that we know as his High Priestly Prayer, recorded in John 17. Our reading of it starts with this solemn warning that the hour approaches so that we must be ready, even as he was ready. What Jesus wanted his disciples and church to recall about his life was the value of his labor for them and his love for God. Jesus desired that both his work and his Father be honored. When your breath slips away the last time, what do you want people to remember?

Jesus' Authority

Your Lord also knew why he'd been given God's authority on earth and what he was supposed to do. His High Priestly prayer continued as Jesus said to his Father, "...you granted [the Son] authority over all people that he might give eternal life to all those you have given him. Now this is eternal life: that they may know you, the only true God, and Jesus Christ, whom you have sent" (Jn. 17:2-3).

Many are bothered because Jesus spoke about himself in the third person. He didn't say, "me" and "I" as he prayed. He referred to himself as "him" or "the Son." But why be troubled by this? Recall that Jesus was praying, yes, but he was also speaking aloud so that the disciples who were gathered around the table might know his most private thoughts regarding his departure from this world. They needed to know what to do next, and in order to find God's plan, they needed to deal with the truths he revealed. His prayer was uttered to the apostles—and through them to the whole church throughout the ages— as well as to the Father in heaven. He spoke in the third person about himself as a tool to communicate thoughts that had to be uttered soon. The hour for such words was swiftly passing.

So what message did Jesus offer Andrew, Matthew, Bartholomew, and us?

Consider a question: Do you have faith in Jesus Christ? If you answer a clear, "Yes," then the Father in heaven gave you to Jesus. You belonged to him eons before you were born, the moment God first considered making you a part of his creation. From before the construction of the universe began, he intended for you to belong to his Son. God gave Jesus authority over you so that he might give you eternal life, just as Christ gives eternal life to everyone God gave him. All the redeemed—you, me, that person over there or down the street—everybody God handed over to Jesus—"red and yellow, black and white, everybody precious in his sight"—have been granted eternal life, because of what Jesus did on the cross. His resurrection is the guarantee of your eternal life. Jesus had authority to do this because God gave him the power, the right, the sanction to permit anybody he chose to live forever in their presence. If you have faith in Jesus, then all of this is a spiritual fact that lies behind the life you live each day. Is this not what the words in John 17:2 mean? Jesus can give everlasting life to anybody he wishes, and those who believe in him must be the ones he chose. Jesus of Nazareth has authority as the Son of God to bestow life forever according to his own desires.

Wow! And he chose *me*? The thought is staggering.

Why should Jesus pick me? I have nothing good or useful that he hasn't given me. I mean, under my own power, by my own choices, I am a miserable person, more so in the eyes of other people than in my own. I cause misery. I also make mistakes left and right. I'm willful, stubborn, selfish and proud. I know me. I do not conduct life as I should, nor do I live by what I know are correct principles. I'm foolish, temperamental, and I *enjoy* being these things! By such sad behavior, I gain a sense of self-control, of power (authority?) over my days, perhaps even my future. I'm an independent cuss. So why would Jesus pick me? My personality is counter to what he desires.

What Jesus Wanted for Himself

We all marvel at the grace our Lord extends to us. We understand how sinful we are, and we delight enough in our transgressions to delay surrendering ourselves as long as possible. When salvation comes by the Lord's mercy, we're caught by surprise and rightly wonder why he should be so thoughtful about us. Yet isn't this the point of our deliverance from sin? Not one of us egotistical, angry, despondent creatures deserve clemency. We merit destruction but receive forgiveness. As Paul reminded the Roman Christians, "...all have sinned and fall short of the glory of God" (Rom. 3:23).

When Jesus exercises his authority and selects a soul for eternal life, a marvelous thing happens. Salvation! In his final public prayer, Jesus impressed upon his disciples the awesome thought of themselves being chosen by him. Don't you want to speculate about how the former fishermen felt? Well, don't. You'll never know. They kept their thoughts that night locked up in their hearts. The closest you can come is to remember how *you* felt when you knew Jesus offered you eternal life.

And what is eternal life? In his departing prayer before the disciples (and the church), Jesus wanted no mistakes about the meaning of eternal life. He defined it in his prayer, and the apostles overheard and remembered and passed on to us what he said: "...this is eternal life: that they may know you, the only true God, and Jesus Christ, whom you have sent" (Jn. 17:2-3). In knowing Jesus, you know he's God's Son and the Father is the only true God. From these two who love you comes the pledge that you'll live forever. When your body breathes its final breath, you'll be present immediately with the glorious God, and when his appointed time arrives, your soul and body will be united in resurrection. This is the Lord's promise of everlasting vibrancy to you. Jesus knew his authority backed up the promise. Do you believe it does? Then act as if it matters. Live with daily hope and joy!

Jesus' Glory

Your Lord knew he succeeded in demonstrating the presence of God on the earth. Now he wanted to return home again to his Father's heavenly presence. He prayed, "I have brought you glory on earth by completing the work you gave me to do. And now, Father, glorify me in your presence with the glory I had with you before the world began" (Jn. 17:4-5). What meaning do you sense in his words? what significance?

I hear a tone of finality in his voice. Jesus had reached an end. He was firm and convinced. He finished the labor he was assigned. One wonders if he was a little homesick for heaven. His words betray an emotion that resonates in me. He's ready to return to his native soil. Think about it. Jesus was from the realm of glory, where his divine instincts made him constantly aware of the Father's presence. While he walked on earth with his self-imposed limitations, with the shortcomings of our human nature, Jesus was restrained from always being alert to God's fellowship or nearness. He was subject to our weaknesses. He had to meditate and pray in order to achieve a sense of the Father's daily companionship. Sometimes, as he lived among humans, God's voice must have been a mere whisper even to the Son. Only occasionally did God speak aloud to our Lord, as when he spoke at the baptism and the transfiguration. On this blue globe, Jesus Christ was a wandering Aramean like Abraham and Jacob, a sojourner away from home, outside his natural element. Having completed his redeeming labor, he was ready to return to the glory he knew before being born in Bethlehem.

I hear a wistful longing in my Lord's voice, and I understand because I've rambled far from home, too.

A certain man wandered in a wilderness until it felt like his home. One day he met two strange beings named Fear and Disease. He asked them where they were going.

"We're on the way to a city," Disease answered.

"What will you do there?"

"We'll kill thousands of people," Disease answered.

The wandering man was uncertain if he should say more, then dared to ask if Disease was to do all the work.

"O, no!" Fear responded with delight in his voice. "My friend will destroy only a few hundred. I'll do the rest!"

Then the wanderer was himself struck by Fear. As the strangers walked slowly toward a setting sun, he felt very much alone in the wasteland where he'd chosen to make his home. He sat and cried while darkness fell.

As a human being, Jesus must have felt the same weight as the wanderer in this story. He'd been faced with people's illness, misery, worry, hopelessness and despair. Everywhere he traveled he was met by the blind, deaf, and lame. He healed bodies and souls. His ministry had taken a toll on his heart, surely. As you feel bleak when you watch videos of starving children and refugees from war or natural disaster, Jesus must have felt crushed at times. No matter how many people he helped, the needs never disappeared! Yet another person would seek love or the finger of miracle or words of compassion. *Who touched my robe?* The power went out from Jesus again and again and again. How drained his years on earth must have left him. No wonder he was eager to return home to the glory of heaven and the soothing presence of his Father!

Do you hear all of what Jesus said? In his prayer, he talked openly with God about being with him *before the world began.* Jesus existed before he was born in the village of Bethlehem! What he was like before history began is a mystery, and when you think too much about it, you're confused. Jesus' pre-existence is puzzling. After all, he's divine as well as human. The point is: you cannot always think about him as only a human being. He is God's Son from eternity to eternity. He shared divine glory with the Father before he ever arrived among us. How awesome! How grand! How amazing! What mystery!

Jesus knew he'd shown God's presence to humanity. "I have brought you glory on earth by completing the work you gave me to do." Yes, only a few people understood. Twelve disciples, and they didn't always comprehend the significance of what he did and said. Others like the man from Arimathea were secretive supporters of his work. Dear friends, such as the Bethany trio openly helped him. Jesus knew people who not only accepted him as God's Son, the revelation of the Father, but also he had loved ones who accepted him as a person like themselves. He understood, too, how quickly the work was coming to an end at Golgotha. Since his mortal work was now finished, since his hour had come, he asked the Father to return him to his heavenly majesty. What did Jesus want for himself? He wanted to go home and receive back the splendor he shared with the Father from all eternity.

Writing about our human attempt to contemplate
Jesus' eternal glory, D. Martyn Lloyd-Jones suggested in
The Assurance of Our Salvation,

> "You do not start with the babe in Bethlehem, that was
> not the beginning of his life. He *came* into this world, he
> was not born into it in the way that everybody else has
> been born into it. He came from the glory. He entered into
> this world from another world, and what he himself says
> here is precisely what is said everywhere else in Scripture,
> that he came out of the eternal, everlasting glory of the
> Godhead."

Jesus wanted to return to the place where his journey
began. How normal his desire was! Like you and me, he
longed for his closest kindred—the Father and the Spirit.

After your long trip, you see the gate in front of your
lighted home and remember who awaits you. Kitchen
smells approach you as you step onto the walk. Time
away was filled with memorable companions, but in a few
heartbeats, you'll be where you belong.

Surely, this joy is what Jesus anticipated as he prayed
to receive the glory he'd known when he was in constant
communion with the Father, a communion never to be
interrupted by the relentless, repeated demands of his
important mission to earth. Home to glory! to happiness!
to fellowship no longer made sporadic by human need or
our limitations!

What Jesus Wanted for Himself

Do you honor Jesus' work along with his Father? You understand the auspicious hour to which he came. He endured the cross and brought God's glory to the most horrible of places, a grave. Jesus exercised authority on earth so that you may have eternal life. You were given to him by the Father; your faith in him is evidence of it. Jesus' success in showing the Father's glory on earth is now perceived in the glory he shares with the Father in his native environment. You understand what he wanted for himself: *Jesus wanted to see his work and his Father honored.*

This was Christ's final desire during his ministry to humanity. Few people in the first century respected his will, and they were confused about God. People continue to dishonor Jesus' ministry and ignore the Father in favor of images imposed upon him from imagination. Jesus is lauded for wisdom and compassion, smart teachings and loving deeds. Yet hearts don't bow easily to him. People decline to surrender obedience or reverence. Are you such a person? Have you seen the Father in the Son? Do you treasure who they are and what they did for you, what they do for you now?

Analyze yourself. Do you venerate Christ as Master? As you consider the Father, what do you respect in him that allows you to stick by the principles he taught you through his Son? Does the prospect of eternity with God and his Son improve your behavior today?

To serve the King of kings, your conduct must become circumspect, righteous. Are you mixed up in conflicts where no Christian ought to be embroiled? Dare you change your life's scenery to blend in and never allow your Christ-inspired morality to shine?

Expressing honor for God is a matter of activity. What you spend your waking hours accomplishing displays clearly the respect you have for the Father and Son. How do you want people to remember you? What are the best expressions of your character? Are you answering Jesus' prayer for himself as he hopes you'll answer? Do you honor his work along with his Father in heaven? You can only show your response by the person you are, the things you do, the places you go, and the words you say.

What will be the legacy of your life?

Chapter Three

Separated from the World

THE RENOWN PREACHER of the First Presbyterian Church, Pittsburgh, Clarence Edward Macartney, visited Geneva and searched for John Calvin's burial place. He wished to pay his respects to the reformation leader who's revered by Presbyterians. Beside a quiet lake, Macartney found an ornate tombstone but discovered it was the monument of the Duke of Brunswick, about whom he knew nothing. As he walked around the lakeshore, Macartney finally found Calvin's grave shaded by a lovely cypress tree. A simple headstone one foot high with the initials "J. C." carved into the stone marked the grave of the noted theologian.

The preacher from Pennsylvania marveled at the difference between the two shrines. One proclaimed the worldly glory of a forgotten lord, and the other spoke quietly of the humble glory of a faithful disciple, whose witness for Christ nurtures God's people five centuries after his death.

In John 17, Christ's prayer continued, now focusing on his disciples, but in its application, it touches you and me as well. In his petition, I find a helpful reminder about the things that make our Christian living distinctive in the present world. The Lord spoke with his Father about this distinctiveness. *He prayed for the disciples to be separated from the world.* The disconnection of believers from their environment deserves closer inspection. So let's see what our Savior meant regarding his people's separation from the world.

Revelation

Jesus revealed God's name and power to the disciples. As he prayed, "I have revealed you to those whom you gave me out of the world. They were yours; you gave them to me and they have obeyed your word. Now they know that everything you have given me comes from you" (Jn. 17:6-7).

The *New International Version* says, "I have revealed *you...*" In Greek, an additional word is included in the sentence. I think a better translation would be "I have revealed your *name...*" The translators apparently felt the Greek phrase *your name* indicated God's person, and it's true: the word *name* did signal the power and prestige of an individual in the ancient world. To act in someone's name meant that you should be accorded the same welcome and deference others gave the person himself. It's not incorrect to translate the phrase simply as "I revealed you..." But I see in the two words *your name* a stronger emphasis than the translators saw. Jesus told the Father that he'd made the power and presence of God— his personal being and authority—clearly known to the disciples. Christ revealed God's dynamic activity in the human realm, and this awesome character of God was discerned and accepted by some who knew Jesus, those whom the Father had given him out of the world, the disciples.

A reason why Jesus entered the human realm, a major motive for his coming into this world, was the display of God's name among humans. When God was visible in nature alone, people could quietly deny his image within themselves. As the apostle Paul explained to the Roman Christians, "...since the creation of the world God's invisible qualities—his eternal power and divine nature— have been clearly seen, being understood from what has been made, so that men are without excuse" (Rom. 1:20). The apostle declared that people knew God but refused to acknowledge or thank him. As a result, their hearts darkened. Revelation of the divine character in nature is insufficient for people to become convinced of God's benevolence toward those who love him. They don't see the display of his potent name, the one who is almighty and saves, nor is the Lord shown to humanity in religious laws. As Paul explained to the Romans,

> Now we know that whatever the law says, it says to those who are under the law, so that every mouth may be silenced and the whole world held accountable to God. Therefore no one will be declared righteous in his sight by observing the law; rather, through the law we become conscious of sin.
>
> Romans 3:19-20

What religious legalism reveals isn't the person of God, the name and authority of the Father, but the presence of human depravity. Our religious observances and even our rituals bring us only so close to God as our sins will allow us to approach, and the distance between him and us is great, as great as our sins. It took Jesus Christ's entrance into the human realm for our souls to perceive the Name, the potent presence and person of God. As Jesus said, "I have revealed you to those whom you gave me out of the world" (Jn. 17:6).

People could try to elevate themselves as masters of their own fates, at least in their private thoughts. Sin is always a choice of what you want over what other people need or what God asks. Selfish choice leads to deeds of arrogance and words of defiance even while you stand before God's gaze. Jesus came among us so that we could see clearly God's eyes and his frown, then we might surrender our pride. The man from Nazareth revealed the Father in heaven to those on earth whom God had given him. Throughout their lives, the disciples were inhabitants of this world, and he showed them what is good and truly glorious—the Father in heaven!

Recall that Jesus spoke his prayer only minutes before going out to Gethsemane where his looming death drove him into an even more anguished time of petition, but his prayers at that time would be in private. For now, he spoke his prayer aloud for all his followers to overhear, yet the context was still the long evening's harrowing discussion of his death around a table strewn with bread crumbs and empty glasses from the initial Lord's Supper. What an awesome setting for his reminder that he spoke as the representative of the divine Name!

Jesus made it very plain to the disciples that he stood on the brink of what Max Lucado called the "canyon of death." Lucado described the awesome gorge in these words: "It is a desolate canyon. The dry ground is cracked and lifeless. A blistering sun heats the wind that moans eerily and stings mercilessly. Tears burn and words come slowly as visitors to the canyon are forced to stare into the ravine. The bottom of the crevice is invisible, the other side unreachable. You can't help but wonder what is hidden in the darkness. And you can't help but long to leave" (*God Came Near: Chronicles of the Christ*). Death prowled near to Jesus as he prayed.

Having helped the disciples grapple with the imminent crucifixion, Jesus used his prayer to back them up from the precipice for a moment. They needed to discern the whole purpose for his coming into the human realm. They knew he was God in human form, but why? To reveal the genuine personality of the Father. The disciples were the privileged ones. They'd been given to Jesus by the Father so that they might perceive the truth about the creative and sovereign Lord, the God of their ancestors. Jesus revealed God's name and power to the disciples, and the revelation was about to be delivered in the dark framework of Christ's dying breath. God himself was about to die. An awesome thought!

Once again, Jesus' prayer mentioned that his followers were people God gave him out of the world. The disciples were God's gift to Christ, just as you and I are God's gift to his Son. Earlier in the evening when Jesus prayed aloud in the upper room, his first followers had indicated how knowing Jesus improved them. According to the Gospel of John, the disciples said, "Now we can see that you know all things and that you do not even need to have anyone ask you questions. This makes us believe that you came from God" (Jn. 16: 30). The Father had convinced them through Jesus' words and deeds. Their knowledge of the divine had enlarged. O, progress in the pursuit of the one true God!

Jesus now expressed his personal opinion of the disciples. He told the Father in heaven, "They were yours; you gave them to me and they have obeyed your word. Now they know that everything you have given me comes from you" (Jn. 17:6b-7). He knew the disciples were his bequest from God, and they had perceived how the relationship they enjoyed with him was a gift from the Father to them. So Jesus summed up their relationship as he prayed aloud to the Father. How his followers were comforted! They belonged to God, who granted them to Jesus his Son. What better relationship might they ever expect in this world?

"It's a very good thing God chose me *before* I was born," British preacher Charles Spurgeon supposedly said, "because he wouldn't have picked me *afterwards!*"

Like Spurgeon and like the disciples, you may wonder why God would ever give you to Jesus. *Why pick me?* But the truth is, by your faith in Christ, you know God has called you to live differently than the world at large lives. The Father gave you to his Son, and he wants you to conduct yourself as Jesus did. If you're to live up to this high calling, won't you have to become separated from the world? Won't you need to alter the character of your conduct among human beings who don't perceive the revelation of God in Jesus Christ? I believe this is what Jesus wanted the disciples to perceive as he prayed with them in the upper room.

Acceptance

As the prayer of John 17 continues, we learn more about the disciples and ourselves. We discover that Jesus' devotees obeyed his teachings, which had come from God, just as everything Jesus possessed was granted by his heavenly Father. Listen to what he prayed: "...I gave them the words you gave me and they accepted them. They knew with certainty that I came from you, and they believed that you sent me" (Jn. 17:8).

Peter, Matthew and Nathaniel, along with their compatriots in the murky light of the upper room, had now grappled with Jesus' teachings for years. They'd been confused and uncertain, disbelieving and believing again, struggling all the time to know who Jesus was and what he wanted. Over long nights of conversation, standing in the background while he healed people, the disciples saw what he could accomplish. They observed his sorrows, compassions, confrontations, and his rejections. Across those hurried days of instruction, Jesus' disciples learned what he wanted them to know. Their insight wasn't perfect and would yet be sorely tried and re-worked in hours, days, years ahead, but the disciples understood Christ gave them the words God gave him. They accepted the words as the divine message to humanity. They were convinced Jesus came to them from God.

By fits and starts, they perceived of Jesus as God, and although their insights must yet be matured, applied and proclaimed, Jesus knew they understood at last who he was, where he was from, what he was doing, and why. At least, they held the germ of the truth, the seed that would sprout, root, enlarge and reproduce a hundredfold. Jesus' disciples obeyed his teachings, and they were persuaded that the good news was from God.

Here's where we begin to see a reason you and I are separated from the world around us. We learn, as did the disciples, to behave as God wants all people to behave. We become Christlike as we're trained in the truth of the gospel. Jesus teaches us who the Father is and what he wants from us. Jesus reveals how we must improve, what must happen to us in order for us to enter the life heaven has planned for those who are given to the Christ. Yet nobody among us acts as we're supposed to act. We need God's help. Jesus teaches us what to do, and when we accept his teachings, applying them to our lives as he applied them to his life, then we become different than the people among whom we live.

However, it is the Spirit of God who has taken up residence in our souls who truly applies Jesus' teachings to our behavior. Living by God's standards now that we possess faith in Jesus, you and I—like the first disciples—are separated from the rest of humanity, from the world and its norms and criteria. People without faith in Christ Jesus live as they please, choosing what they want, going where they desire, following whatever flag is raised before them, rallying to the cries of worldly concerns, lusts and ambitions. But the Christian's flag flies from the cross of a humble servant! Standing there before him, we're made different, better, discerning, holy. This is only partly our doing. It's primarily God's gift to Jesus. Our becoming like Christ is a blend of humble response below, on terra firma, and the gracious benediction from above, from heaven. It's a mixture of meek discovery with generous sanction. "For God so loved the world that he gave his one and only Son, that whoever believes in him shall not perish but have eternal life" (Jn. 3:16). We're separated from the world by God's grace through the accepting response we make to his kindness toward us in Jesus. God gives us his blessing, and we receive it thankfully.

A missionary to Asia dined with military officials. An officer asked a rather impolite question: "Why don't you missionaries go home? Look after your religious concerns there!"

The missionary responded, "If you were commissioned to take your battleship to a certain place, would you obey or not?"

The impertinent one snapped upright. "Ordered to go, we shall go, even if every ship sinks and every sailor drowns!"

"Right!" the missionary agreed. "I also have orders. God tells me, 'Go! Preach the gospel everywhere.'"

Acceptance means obedience, and your obedience to Jesus Christ, and mine, begins a process of making you and me different from the surrounding world. The world isn't compliant with what Jesus wants, but we are! We're separated from the world by submission to the Lord.

Why can't the world submit to God's revealed way in Christ? What keeps people from acceptance and obedient service? An unappreciated reality. A reality that separates humans like us from the Almighty in the first place. *Sin.* So what's sin? It has numerous subtle components. Self-indulgence is one aspect of it. A person who lives in a fallen world—and this world is a fallen, unnatural world, one that God did not plan, but is of human fabrication—

must favor self over others. She will choose the happiness of herself and her child over the comfort of another woman and her child. He will apply his most labored efforts to the safety of his household but give nothing or nearly nothing to improve the welfare of a neighbor. Self-indulgence leads to seeking pleasure for oneself, and one's dear hearts, to the exclusion of concern for people round the corner. Why else would somebody go camping in a food-stuffed motor home costing tens of thousands of dollars without a thought for the elderly man next door who eats almost nothing every day because his pension check won't cover both food and medicine? Such self-indulgence, or another act similar to it, happens daily in all neighborhoods. Unacknowledged sin, together with a struggle against sins that are acknowledged, is part of what separates the world and the Christian. People who do wrong and enjoy it don't mingle easily with those who do right and like it.

For this reason, if you choose to accept what the Savior teaches about the loving Father, and if you want to be obedient to his revealed way of godliness, you have to become ready to experience a cold shoulder from friends who care nothing for Jesus. Acceptance brings obedience, and obedience brings the need to endure, because those who do not accept or obey will not understand you anymore. Separation develops of its own accord. It's almost a living entity. The believer cannot stop it without forsaking his Lord, which he cannot bring himself to do. Neither can unbelieving people stop the development of separation from Christians, because they won't surrender their self-opinion or other sacred but mistaken beliefs (mistaken from a Christian perspective).

In 1912, the Terra Nova Expedition to the Antarctic perished in snow and ice. A member of the expedition, Robert Falcon Scott, kept a diary which was later found and published. In one entry, his pen scrawled, "Had we lived, I should have had a tale to tell of the hardihood, endurance, and courage of my companions which would have stirred the heart of every Englishman. These rough notes and our dead bodies must tell the tale." The endurance and agony of the expedition's members, alone and isolated from their supplies by eleven frozen and blizzard-infested miles speaks clearly of what separation from help and hope can do.

Christians have found divine help and hope in Jesus Christ, and they endure the rigors of an isolated life. They accept their Lord's vision of what the world should be, what it will be. In acceptance comes the resolve to persist, but also in acceptance comes the genesis of separation from a world that lies so close at hand, but so far away in trust and understanding. People who don't believe Jesus can't comprehend why you live the strange, circumspect life you lead. Their criteria for good living is so different from your God-given principles. Can you expect anything but painful separation?

Preservation

Jesus also prayed for the disciples' preservation in the world. As he said to his Father, "I pray for them. I am not praying for the world, but for those you have given me, for they are yours" (Jn. 17:9). Since the world opposed Jesus, he went to the cross for the sake of those whom the Father had given him, and as he left this world, Jesus asked God to preserve his trusting people, the disciples, you and me and all Christian believers who lived before us and who will come after us during the history of the church. Jesus wanted his success upheld and carried on.

Being given to Christ, you were chosen for him by God. In other words, you were *predestined* to travel with Jesus in faith and obedience. A lot of people have trouble with this idea, but think of it this way: It's like taking a cruise. The owner of the ship picked your destination, planned your route, chose what happens onboard ship, and decided what ports of call will be visited. His mailing invited you to come along on the cruise. If you accept the offer—if you receive Jesus as Savior and obey him—then he guaranteed you'll make the trip safely and enjoy the cruise. You didn't treat God's offer like junk mail. Instead of going to the garbage can with it, you accepted Jesus. You bought the ticket for the price of faith. Now you're checking in at the dock with your boarding pass! You're one of those given to Jesus, one of those who chose him. Yet you were also picked out of a computer database as a person who'd accept the offer and come aboard. Here's predestination and free will at work together!

(Please, don't press the analogy too far, but I think you see the point being made. No discrepancy exists between freedom of the human will and divine choice of whom God will save.)

By his upper room prayer for the church, our Savior promised preservation to all whom God gave him. They responded with acceptance and obedience. So Jesus asked God to sustain them when he left this world. He now wants you to carry on his work, and so he asks God to defend you, care for you, safeguard you, preserve you by a divine protection.

JESUS PRAYED that the disciples would be separated from the world. Isn't this how you and I find our distinctive life as Christians? Living in this world without being caught up in its silliness or vanity, we serve our Lord well because we divide ourselves from the proud human search for a temporary glory. Our refusal to run after the world's trinkets, the momentary satisfactions of the flesh or the heart, makes us stand apart from the bulk of humanity. Jesus reveals God's name and power in your holy conduct. He asks you to accept and to obey his teachings, although they cause you to become different from other people, whose loyalties are to earth's empire. Jesus promises to preserve you while you walk his solitary path in the world.

You're called to separate from the world's selfish and worthless habits. Will you give Jesus what he wants?

Chapter Four

Protected in the World

A SENTENCE FROM AN OLD POEM comforts me. The poet
was James Freeman Clarke.

> Beneath the shadow of the Great Protection,
> The soul sits, hushed and calm.
>
> *The Shadow*, Stanza 2

For me, the sentence speaks about security and shelter in
Christ. Throughout my life's ups and downs, I've known a
defending shadow. I hope your soul has also been hushed
and calmed, knowing you sit in the Protector's shade.

As he prepared to exit the world, Jesus fretted over his
followers' welfare. In the quiet upper room, he prayed
that the disciples might be protected in the world. We
should investigate what his uneasiness means for us.

Glory for Jesus

Do you hear what Jesus said to the Father? "All I have
is yours, and all you have is mine. And glory has come to

me through them" (Jn. 17:10). Jesus was glorified, as he should be. What amazes me is the *source* of his glory. Christ was glorified through the disciples.

Put yourself in the upper room. Feel what the dinner companions felt. Jesus said God owned everything: "All I have is yours..." He admitted how every valuable thing in his life belonged to the Father in heaven. Nothing startles in this statement. The disciples would have agreed with the idea in reference to themselves. Every precious thing in their lives belonged to God. Their children, spouses, homes, and employment. Some had learned the craft of fishing from their fathers and made a good living at it when Jesus called them to become "fishers of men." One was an enterprising tax collector when summoned to discipleship. They weren't men of substance as the world sees wealth, but the disciples were people with cherished assets. Each one felt blessed by heaven. They were avid supporters of the Nazarene, discovering in him the long-desired Messiah, their Savior and Lord. He was their highest blessing from the Father. They wouldn't be startled when Jesus said to God, "All I have is yours..." They were thankful for divinely given prosperity, too.

Then Jesus declared an audacious truth. The whole of what God possessed belonged to *him*! "...all you have is mine..." Who'd claim to hold all God owned? Not you, nor me, and certainly not the disciples. God is infinite, yet

Jesus became finite. He broke into the human realm, and when the disciples related to him, they saw flesh and blood, a man like them. He hungered, fatigued, grew irritated when people wanted more and more but gave back little or nothing. Jesus was valued as a human before he was recognized as God. Half a lifetime later, after years of proclamation and meditation, the apostle John was able to open his gospel with the thought of Jesus as the pre-existent divine Word: "The Word became flesh and made his dwelling among us. We have seen his glory..." (Jn. 1:14a). This recognition was still in the future. For the moment, in the upper room, preparing for Jesus' departure to heaven, the disciples knew Christ as more like them than like God. For the man from Nazareth to claim every one of God's possessions for himself sounded impudent, overconfident. The claim intruded on their relationship with Jesus. Either he was God's Son or he was out of his mind! They must decide, and decide right now. Would they continue to follow someone so audacious as to claim for himself all God owned?

Time was crucial. Jesus made sure the disciples knew what he meant. The next hour or two would produce betrayal, arrest and trial. His death approached on fluttering wings. If he failed to get his thought across plainly, unmistakably and immediately, the disciples may never fully comprehend who he was, why he came, what he taught, and how he accomplished his mission. The future proclamation of the gospel lay suspended between the final supper he instituted and the final breath he was to gasp. Jesus was about to die, and so he pointed out a daring truth which the disciples must not forget. All God's possessions belonged to him! The most expensive treasure of the Father was *the disciples themselves*!

In his prayer, Jesus announced,

> I pray for them. I am not praying for the world, but for those you have given me, for they are yours. All I have is yours, and all you have is mine. And glory has come to me through them.
>
> *John* 17:9-10

What an affluent gift the disciples were! They had already glorified Jesus on earth. He himself announced it! "And glory has come to me through *them*."

Imagine how the disciples felt. What had they done to glorify Jesus? Their morals were imperfect; they were still developing into *his* morality. John, who recorded the Lord's prayerful words, must certainly have remembered the painful failure of his brother, his mother and himself. They'd sought a privileged, powerful seat next to Jesus in his kingdom. Christ asked if they could tipple from the cup he drank. They dared to say they could. In their own minds, James and John were confident of struggling for human redemption as Jesus struggled for it. But he took them down a peg when he announced that the brothers would one day drink his beverage and be baptized as he was about to be plunged beneath the murky water of the cross. However, places of honor weren't his to give. How John saw Jesus and himself was inadequate for what he must yet do in his life.

Each disciple had such tales of failure to tell, and more failure in Jesus' service would arrive soon. They made mistakes. They failed him. How could they have already radiated his glory? How could they show his majesty to the world? Imperfection and sinful humanity should have precluded success. Yet somehow they'd glorified Christ. He said so! To his Father in heaven! They overheard his intimate prayer. The achievement must be true. But how? They didn't understand. They marveled at the thought during a silence filled with confusion and puzzlement. How had they glorified Jesus?

Surely, you too can hope to reflect Jesus so that others might know him and enjoy him forever. You don't think so? You say you're morally corrupt. Lies escaped your lips. Fears crushed your testimony about Christ. You tried to walk a narrow path, but footpaths near it drew you into unfruitful endeavors. You wasted time, life and resources in abundance. Why would Jesus be glorified in any triumph you achieved in the convoluted walk you've taken? How can anyone see in your behavior a picture of goodness, happiness, patience, the grace of God? You mocked him by the bad seeds you planted—ambition, discord, jealousy. You sowed them all! How can you glorify Jesus?

Remember: The original disciples were no different than you, and Jesus declared that they glorified him. Recall this, too. Throughout the high priestly prayer, Jesus prayed for all his people. Thaddeus, Martha, Simon the Zealot and Mary Magdalene. And *you*! Somehow you brought honor and glory to Jesus' name. Look for the evidence. It's there. Jesus saw it. You're a valued treasure God gave his Son. Your faith in him proves it. So raise higher your self-image! It isn't as ugly as you think. Jesus knows this. As you have glorified him, glorify him still more by deliberately choosing to live in his way.

Guarding for the Disciples

Do you hear what else Jesus asked God? Your Savior prayed these thoughts:

> "I will remain in the world no longer, but they are still in the world, and I am coming to you. Holy Father, protect them by the power of your name—the name you gave me—so that they may be one as we are one. While I was with them, I protected them and kept them safe by that name you gave me..."
>
> John 17:11-12*a*

During past years, as he toured Galilee and Judea with the disciples, Jesus taught God's way. He entrusted them with service in his name. He used the forcefulness of his own personality to keep them safe when Pharisees and others criticized them. Jesus' divine authority was built on the foundation of the Father's name—his authority—and he'd guarded the disciples. Neither Jesus nor his first followers failed in their combined mission of instruction and truth, compassion and love. A continued shielding—a guarding, a protection—was required for his people. Otherwise, the mission would deteriorate. The disciples weren't leaving the world. Only Christ departed. They had belonged to the Father before they were given to Jesus. Now God should renew his responsibility for them. So Jesus asked him to renew his guardianship over their followers.

Consider how they felt overhearing this part of Jesus' prayer. Sorrow flooded their hearts. Jesus insisted he was leaving the world. What could it mean except death? He claimed to be the Protector, using God's name, authority and power. After he left, what would become of them? Sorrow flowed into anxiety. Worry flooded across fear! Tumbling over one another, the devotees' emotions congealed. So hard to think straight! Gloom filled the upper chamber in a borrowed house. The Lord called them friends because they knew his plans. How could he intend to desert them? Would he really go away? Where? Why? How could they pick up their old occupations? Questions about fishing on Lake Galilee again entered a mind or two. A whispered panic skipped across the dining table. How to reach safety? Doors and windows were locked! But why run from Jesus? Without him who wanted to leave this awful room? He was their Protector.

As Shakespeare once wrote, "Extreme fear can neither fight nor fly." In darkness on a somber night, the disciples filled with anxiety, alarm, dread. Leaving the upper room and walking to Gethsemane, their acute fear lessened, but during his betrayal and arrest, a resurgent terror impelled them to desert Jesus in the garden. They hesitated to tag along in the shadows to either Caiaphas' house or the Roman Praetorium. Jesus found himself almost alone by the time he reached the hill called the Skull. But, for the closing quarter-hour in the upper room, his friends shook with worry. An undreamed nightmare built a foundation inside them. Without Jesus? How? How could they serve God when his Anointed One vanished?

Have you had a close friend who understood you? He knew your mind on all matters, your sentiments in all situations. He read you like an open book. He was aware of your need for support, and when you should be left alone. Then one day your friend announced, "I'm leaving town. I'm moving south and retiring." Suddenly, you're secluded from the rest of the world. He won't be here to comfort you when injured or to inform you with sharp perceptions. The most sensitive person you know, on whom you depend, has surrendered your association, seeking private benefit while permitting your ship to founder. Who'll be your strength and good judgment now? Whose opinions will inform your wisdom?

How unguarded you felt! How defenseless! You were exposed, vulnerable to the mistakes you knew you'd make without his assistance. This is how the disciples felt when Jesus' prayer notified them of his departure. They felt the solitude left to them in a dangerous world. They were lonesome! Abandoned! Forlorn! Alone! Such moods slid around the table.

But praise God! Jesus asked the Father to protect the disciples in his absence. They weren't to be alone after all. The Father would use his name to guard them. Indeed, his Spirit was soon to fill each follower with comfort and counsel. They weren't fully persuaded what the Spirit's presence should mean, but they understood this from Jesus' prayer: They weren't orphans, nor destitute! The Father would keep them.

How? Jesus traced the means of divine protection at the end of his sentence about their security: "Holy Father, protect them by the power of your name—the name you gave me—so that they may be one as we are one" (Jn. 17:11). *So they can be one as we're one!* Jesus told the fearful disciples where fortification is found under God's grace. In the church's fellowship, its oneness, its unity.

Practiced by a lone person, Christianity is neither fully nor faithfully observed. Although your individualism is permissible, it isn't the substance of Christian life. You must be a disciple who stands on his or her own feet. Yet you must also be a Christian among other followers. We're the body of Christ together! Christianity is no Lone Ranger religion. Jesus asked God to protect the disciples so that their relationship with one another—and in time with other believers—might shield them. Jesus' name, the *Christ*, along with a believer's name, *Christian*, represent the church's unity. *So they can be one as we're one!* The goal of guarding the disciples is achieved throughout time in the binding together of God's faithful servants.

Among the Puritans a proverb arose from the pen of Richard Baxter: "In necessary things, unity; in doubtful things, liberty; in all things, charity." Here's the Christian way. Believers live together in agreement. They exist as a singular entity, a harmonious body, committed to each other. When they disagree, they maintain unity by consenting to liberty of conscience. They respect every believer's scruples, her ethics, his morality, by showing a forgiving love. Church unity is based in the oneness of the Father, Son, and Holy Spirit. Belonging to the redeemed family of God, Christ's people express oneness through compassion, generosity, forbearance. We fulfill our Lord's final public prayer for the church.

Jesus also addressed God as his *holy* Father. Nowhere else in scripture are these two words combined. Holiness is an attribute of God's person. The Spirit is called holy. We're enjoined to be holy as God is holy. But God as Father is only once called holy (here in John 17:11), and the sentiment was expressed by Jesus the Son. This is a unique designation for God, and it's not often used today by devout Jews or Christians. What might Jesus refer to? How is the Father holy to Jesus?

The basic concept of holiness in the Bible is the idea of separation. Objects are made holy by a ritual designed to establish their detached status. A utensil for use in the Jerusalem temple was made holy by a washing ceremony; then it was restricted in how it was used. A bowl, once set apart for offering a sacrifice, must always be treated as a sacred tool to hold something employed in the worship of God. When no longer usable in such a fashion, it was destroyed. Some gifts to the temple were devoted to God, made holy and distinct, and they were destroyed when donated. At its root, holiness is an absolute surrender.

Applying these thoughts to the relationship between the Father and the Son, perhaps Jesus was saying to God, "You're thoroughly committed to my welfare and to the welfare of those whom I redeem. You're set apart as our holy Parent. You alone protect us. Please remember this as I come home to you, and keep our family safe."

Doesn't this thrill you? You're guarded by God's name! His presence and authority keep you secure. You aren't deserted, without aid in a harsh world. Since Jesus left the human realm, you've been protected by the Holy One, by the Father in heaven. Can't you allow relief to fill you? Trust God's love. He's the sentry at your soul's door. He's your strong defender!

Gloom for One Disciple

Do you also hear what Jesus lamented in his prayer? In regret, he told the Father, "None has been lost except the one doomed to destruction so that Scripture would be fulfilled" (Jn. 17:12b). Jesus labored past snag and hurdle to preserve each disciple who learned how to serve God through his ministry. Now, gloom bubbled up because of one disciple. Jesus was sorrowful over Judas Iscariot, who was soon to betray him. The betrayer obscured Jesus' thoughts on this last evening with his friends. Judas' treachery shaded the Lord's soul with dreariness as he stepped up to the cross. Christ acknowledged the gloom caused by one disciple.

His suffering wasn't only at the hands of those who hated and distrusted him; it was also at the hands of those who loved him and were loved in return. Gloom awaited Judas when he realized what he'd done, and the shadow would make him commit suicide. Yet the unhappiness already engulfed Jesus. He loved Iscariot and lamented this singular disciple who'd soon hand him over to the authorities. Jesus the realist understood how the turncoat was doomed to destruction. Scripture predicted it.

What scripture? Perhaps Psalm 41:9 weighed on Jesus' heart as he spoke this awful sentence about his betrayer to the only one who understood, his heavenly Father. The psalm says...

> Even my close friend, whom I trusted,
> he who shared my bread,
> has lifted up his heel against me.
>
> Psalm 41:9

Earlier this night, Jesus explained how someone among the disciples was going to be disloyal. He said, "I am not referring to all of you; I know those I have chosen. But this is to fulfill the scripture: 'He who shares my bread has lifted up his heel against me'" (Jn. 13:18). He referred to Psalm 41 then. Now in his prayer to the Father, he mentioned the poem again. Our Lord's sorrow was great, because he knew ahead of time that the traitor was someone who loved him. What pain bored into his soul!

Two centuries before Jesus lived, Titus Maccius Plautus said, "There are occasions when it is undoubtedly better to incur loss than to make gain." Thinking about Judas and Jesus, I suspect the Lord came to realize no more could be gained with Iscariot. Their relationship had broken down. Judas no longer agreed with him. The disciple worried needlessly, and greedily, about the cost of oil a woman used to anoint Jesus. Undoubtedly, there were more telltale signs that the relationship was dead. They weren't visible to the rest of the band, but clear to Jesus, who was always perceptive about those around him. Jesus came to believe this was a time to incur loss, and his pain was evident in his prayer.

The longer I've meditated on the sufferings of Christ, the more I've understood how far-reaching his agonies were. We remember his endurance of mockery by bored and brutal Roman soldiers. Physical and mental abuse piled up against his heart. Spikes, splinters and a spear were an equal terror and an awesome misery.

Jesus' suffering began before his final morning. When he cried for Jerusalem while he descended the mountain road toward the city, Jesus' heart broke because of all who hadn't listened, who didn't care. He also accepted the disciples' frequent misunderstanding of his words. In a stalwart, distressed mood, he repeated his lessons with hope for them. Whenever Peter hit the mark of faith and obedience, Jesus rejoiced, but time and again the big fisherman brought him chagrin and gloom. Even while he was dying, Jesus was uncertain anyone except the beloved disciple and his mother, with a few unnamed others, remained faithful. I'm not surprised by Jesus' melancholy lament over Judas. The disciple's failure was one grief in a long line of heartaches that he endured during his life.

The apostle Paul reminded Christians in Corinth how a believer's privation, sadness, and misfortune integrate with the miseries of Christ. He wrote,

> ...just as the sufferings of Christ flow over into our lives, so also through Christ our comfort overflows. If we are distressed, it is for your comfort and salvation; if we are comforted, it is for your comfort, which produces in you patient endurance of the same sufferings we suffer.
>
> 2 *Corinthians* 1:5-6

As Jesus' depressions and sorrows resulted in reassurance and solace for the apostle, so Paul's endurance of pain for Christian friends delivered encouragement to them. Also, their relief created good cheer and contentment in other faithful followers of the Lord. The church's unity displays itself in shared anguish, too.

A truth meets us in the gloom associated with Judas Iscariot: No great work is ever accomplished without loss. Sacrifices abound when you attempt the impossible, as Jesus did. Humanity was steeped in sin, and salvation was unlikely. Our hearts were too corrupt to desire God. Our thoughts too selfish to care about the Creator's need for fellowship with his creatures. Yet Jesus cut through the murkiness of our existence with a sharp, shining scalpel. He excised guilt and redeemed the irredeemable. The cost was high. Jesus himself bled, betrayed by one whom he loved sincerely. He acknowledged the gloom reserved for the one disciple who turned away. He protected every follower save this one. Misery at losing Judas would be repeated if he lost *you*. What sorrow! What gloominess! This, too, your Lord bore to the Father in prayer.

IN A SERMON ON CHRIST'S DEATH, John Calvin declared that since Jesus "...has been ordained our Shepherd, he watches over our salvation, in order that we may be secure under his hand and under his protection" (*The Deity of Christ*). We overhear the same truth while Jesus talked openly with the Father about the disciples, about you and me. Shortly before his betrayal and death, Jesus prayed for his disciples to be protected in the world.

Do you believe Jesus prayed this way about you? Then live with confidence in his protection. As the hymn tells you...

> Take it to the Lord in prayer!
> In his arms, he'll take and shield thee,
> Thou wilt find a solace there.
>
> *Joseph Scriven*

Chapter Five

Sanctified in the World

ELBERT HUBBARD wrote in *Leadership* magazine, "If your religion does not change you, then you should change your religion." To me, he exposes a distinctive aspect of Christianity: It changes people for the better! People who choose seriously to follow Jesus find they have to improve how they live. You cannot be a good disciple and conduct yourself like a demon.

A shroud encases the pursuits of some who profess allegiance to Jesus. They claim him as Redeemer, but their religion hasn't much improved their involvements. Cigarettes attract with addictive power. Alcohol robs their best efforts as well as physical health. Yes, the habits are obsessions caused by chemical imbalances in their bodies, but a variety of assistants can be found to lessen or remove such dependency. Weakness experienced in ridding themselves of chemical props happens because they won't surrender control to Christ or to the power he puts in their spirits, his own Holy Spirit. They may be given to him as Savior, but his Lordship escapes their notice. Although they're rescued people, they remain endangered by a former sin that maintains a disruptive link with an unreformed, worldly-minded conduct. Such believers haven't learned the need for sanctification, for being set apart for God's use each day.

In this chapter, we see a similar concern expressed in our Lord's petition for his people. *Jesus prays that his disciples will be sanctified in the world.* He wants us improved from inside out so that we can make the world itself better. As the heart goes, so goes the conduct. Or at least, behavior *should* follow the heart's new allegiance. Let's investigate what Jesus requested for his people.

Happily Troubled

Notice this: *Because of Christ's prayer, you're happily troubled.* When you become serious about faith in Jesus, you discern two amazing truths. You're happier than you used to be, and you're more troubled. A paradox? No, it's a paired experience of the Christian life. The head and tail of a coin. Believers are both happy and troubled.

"I am coming to you now," Jesus prayed to his Father, "but I say these things while I am still in the world, so that they may have the full measure of my joy within them. I have given them your word and the world has hated them, for they are not of the world any more than I am of the world" (Jn. 17:13-14).

Jesus wanted his disciples to be happy. He understood how his exodus from the world was about to create a void in their hearts. No longer would they walk with him beside them visibly. Meals together could now only be real in a spiritual sense, such as the Supper he instituted that night. Even so, he wanted them to find happiness. They were his friends! Jesus wished to share with them *the full measure of his own joy.* That was his phrase. What did he mean by it? While on earth, he knew intimacy with God deeply enough to learn the peace that goes beyond expression in words, and he wanted such happiness for Simon, Thaddeus, Bartholomew, for all disciples.

Jesus also wanted you to have the same measure—the *fullness*—of his personal joy. He asked the Father to give you intimacy with himself. In Christ, you participate in a personal relationship the size of an underground cavern where you can daily draw pure, living water to refresh your soul. The rich flavor of Jesus' happiness spreads across your knowledge of God. It infuses zest into your life. With King David, you relish a liberating experience:

> Restore to me the joy of your salvation
> and grant me a willing spirit, to sustain me.
>
> *Psalm* 51:12

In the Shadow with Jesus

Your life-upgrading faith in Jesus Christ makes the full measure of his joy available to you. Have you felt it? Search your soul for the truth about your belief in him. If your religion hasn't improved you, then improve your religion!

Yet there's another side to being happy in Jesus, and it requires a willing spirit to sustain you. It's the trouble you'll see because you consciously belong to the Lord. As he prayed to his Father, Jesus wanted the disciples—who were in the upper room listening to his prayer—to accept God's message, although they'd be hated because of the approval. The Savior's desire came from his own earthly experience. He endured anger from people who couldn't understand what he told them, nor would they accept the good character they saw in his conduct. They complained about his healings, his teachings, his revelation of the role he played in the drama of salvation. When the disciples went across the world in his name, they'd also be hated, abused, troubled. But! they'd be happy in their troubles because the disciples knew Christ! By the memory of his prayer, they'd understand he hadn't abandoned them. His Spirit would be alive in their spirits, and the effect would be visible to them, if not to the many people before whom they witnessed. His people were going to rejoice in his blessings, and because of the joy he gave, they'd endure their woes well, too. They'd be happily troubled!

During a 1991 interview in *U. S. Catholic* magazine, Stanley Hauerwas said, "Christianity is the proclamation that God gives Christians a gift that they don't know they need. The gift then transforms their lives so that they are trained to want the right things rightly."

Don't you know the truth of this? Hasn't salvation improved your character? What difference has it made in your ordinary conduct? As the song says, "...there's no other way to be happy in Jesus but to trust and obey!" Do you trust? Don't you obey? Aren't you happy? My guess is that you have occasional doubts, moments when life's dreariness or danger produce fear that you may not be the Christian you're called to be. Now remember: Your Savior prayed that this would happen to you. He wants you to stand in the shadow with him, to experience the fragile nature of wholehearted surrender, the brittleness of unreserved obedience. You can't be happy if you don't walk closely with him throughout your life. However, although you're safe, you aren't immune. Pain creeps upon your soul and causes you to shudder as you observe the awesome cost of servanthood. You must walk in the valley of the shadow, too. The shadow of obedience to the cross. You must live a holy, capitulated life—one in which you act as Jesus acted. You must love those who are hard to love, forgive those who are treacherous, and give mercy to those who are ungracious. So expect to be happily troubled. Also, be honest with yourself and Jesus. Would you want to have it any other way?

Suitably Protected

Now, notice this equally marvelous truth: *Because of Christ's prayer, you're suitably protected.* Folks who get serious about their faith in Jesus discover two more spiritual facts. They're protected by a divine hand, and they're protected in a most suitable way. The Lord loves his people too much to leave them unassisted in a hard-bitten world. If they encounter cynicism, their spirits could be devastated or their commitment to God's rule of their lives might lessen. Therefore, as he approached the cross, Jesus pledged himself to seek a suitable protection for you.

"My prayer is not that you take them out of the world," Jesus admitted to the Father, "but that you protect them from the evil one. They are not of the world, even as I am not of it" (Jn. 17:15-16).

Jesus wanted his disciples to be protected against the evil one. In this fallen world, an active force moves with a cunning, malicious intent. He's the evil one, the Lord's immoral and unpleasant opponent, and his goal is to do harm to all God blesses. As Paul clarified for Christians in the Greek city of Thessalonica, "...we wanted to come to you—certainly I, Paul, did, again and again—but Satan stopped us" (1 Thess. 2:17). In whatever way the evil one obstructed the apostle's movements, the adversary's goal was to cut short the blessing God would have sent to the congregation if Paul had visited when he wished.

The evil one wants to hurt you, if you accept Jesus into your life and choose to live by God's revealed standards. You're like George Whitefield who evangelized during religious revivals in colonial era America. He described his life as a sheet of paper given to God: "I have put my soul, as a blank, into the hands of Jesus Christ my Redeemer, and desired him to write upon it what he pleases. I know it will be his own image." If you're also completely devoted to Christ, then you'll need protection just as Whitefield felt he needed divine assistance. Like Cephas, John, Silas, Mark, and every Christian between their time and the twenty-first century, you require protection against the evil one. Be calm in your soul. Jesus already asked his Father to keep you safe! Nothing will happen to you that God cannot turn to good ends. The evil one may be wicked, but in the end he's powerless to do anything except cause a little fuss.

While he prayed aloud in the upper room, knowing his hour had come and his time with his first followers was almost ended, Jesus wanted the disciples to understand that they didn't fit this world anymore. "They aren't of this world," he said aloud to the Father as eleven of the twelve listened around the table. Even as Jesus himself wasn't of the world, the disciples weren't fully part of the earth anymore. The Lord had come from heaven, and as he walked earth's roads, he lived by a holier benchmark, a heavenly paradigm. He acted above the standards of his contemporaries. So many of them felt compromises with unrighteousness were required. They overlooked cruelty and oppression, disgust and greed while pretending to be what they were not, saying good words but doing poor deeds. Jesus Christ wasn't like them. His drummer beat the rhythms of heaven, and he strode the earth without feeling fully akin to it. Having taught Peter, James and John to keep cadence with him, they too must live by new principles instead of the fallen ways of humanity.

Neither are you like earth's fallen ones. Jesus removed you from the world by instructing you in what's right. From him you learned to be compassionate more often than callous, generous rather than stingy, selfless instead of selfish. You discovered what Søren Kierkegaard wrote in his journal: "God creates out of *nothing*. Wonderful, you say. Yes, to be sure, but he does what is still more wonderful: he makes saints out of sinners." You're neither the blameworthy nor immoral person you once were on the road to becoming. You were rescued through the work Jesus of Nazareth did on a splintered cross. You're a new being in him! The tradition by which you understand the world has been changed; the yardstick by which you measure your actions has been made more accurate and dependable. Your new flag bears colors from heaven's kingdom! Yes, you're still learning Jesus' teachings, but as he looks ahead to what you will be, God's Son has already asked his Father to protect you. "My prayer is not that you take them out of the world," Jesus said, "but that you protect them from the evil one." Wow! Doesn't his love amaze you? It astounds me!

Yet how does protection come to us who are happily troubled? In as surprising a manner as come all the gifts of Christian experience. Jesus prayed for it to happen, and you pray, too. "So I say to you," Jesus announced. "Ask and it will be given to you; seek and you will find; knock and the door will be opened to you" (Lk. 11:9). As a father gives healthy food instead of a dangerous snake to his baby, so God answers requests for security.

First, his word is the armor that defends you. Reading scripture every day, you build up a solid understanding of the norms by which you struggle to conduct yourself. Knowing the truth releases you to act according to the customs of heaven instead of human folly. The Bible is your God-given tool for both faith and practice. It teaches you what to believe and what to do.

Second, a regular fellowship within the body of Christ is a guard against moral and spiritual failure. The point of church attendance is not to win Brownie points so that you can one day stand before the great throne and say, "See what I did!" Worship and community life within a congregation are God's established means to keep you suitably protected in a persuasive yet deceptive world. Within the body of Christ, you share the sacraments and are given comfort and inspiration for the next leg of your journey amid the ogres of earth. In the congregation, you have resources for counsel and guidance, wisdom and discretion as you face trials in a world that doesn't care much about you.

Can a suitable protection be as simple as this? Yes! But you have to believe the truth of it and act accordingly. Have you done so? Will you continue to your life's end? God's help is with you, but you must seek it.

Faithfully Sanctified

Now, notice this: *Because of Christ's prayer, you're faithfully sanctified.* Anyone who becomes serious about remaining Jesus' loyal disciple discovers two other truths. They're sanctified, made holy, and they're made virtuous because Jesus remains resolute and reliable both toward them and toward the Father. Your Lord has no desire for your life to be hard, although he recognizes how awkward it will be when you choose his principles over the world's misguidance. For that reason, he's inflexibly focused on the development of your godly character. Jesus knows you'll succeed in Christian life within a world where you don't belong, but only in proportion to your dedication to walk earth as you'd walk heaven. Therefore, he petitions the Father to approve you, to consecrate you to himself. What does Jesus want for you and me?

"Sanctify them by the truth; your word is truth," Jesus prayed to his Father. "As you sent me into the world, I have sent them into the world. For them I sanctify myself, that they too may be truly sanctified" (Jn. 17:17-19).

Back to the Bible! God's word is able to set you apart for his honor and service. Your success as a witness to divine things on earth and as a citizen of heaven demands constant improvements in your character. You still have too much of the world in you! It must be either scoured hard or rinsed mildly out of your soul. This is the job of scripture and Christ's Spirit. As Paul instructed his co-worker Timothy: "All Scripture is God-breathed and is useful for teaching, rebuking, correcting and training in righteousness, so that the man of God may be thoroughly equipped for every good work" (2 Tim. 3:16-17). The words recorded on the thin pages of your Bible in black and red ink contain and elucidate the truth Jesus was charged to tell us. By his instructions, we're sanctified. Once enlightened by the plain words, once consecrated by the lesson from heaven, you're ready to be sent into the world. In proportion to your clarity about Christ's gospel and your candor of conduct in his name, you will succeed in showing the world what Jesus showed it. People will say you're being holier-than-thou, but you'll actually be acting by standards they don't yet understand, the veracity of the almighty God. Do you see why you need the Bible in order to be the person Jesus wants you to be? the one he asks his Father to make you?

Consider how much Jesus wanted the disciples to be holy, to be set apart for God—to live with him and serve him in this collapsing world, as well as in the world to come. His prayer suggested a course of action for the twelve-minus-one disciples. Throughout the evening in the secluded room, they'd wondered what would happen to them if Jesus were to leave. Questions and confusions abounded in their hearts, though the Lord had been preparing them for weeks for this night's arrival and for the imminent, horrible events of tomorrow morning. How could he sway them to renewed confidence?

Rather than loyalty at the crucial moment, the fishers of men were contemplating a return to their familiar boats and nets, but little did they suspect their return would be to renewed days of humdrum, painful labor, and nights to remember dreams they once cherished but had lost. They needed brought back into God's presence, but to be in God's presence requires you to be holy, to be consecrated to him, to be thoroughly committed to God in heart, mind and behavior. So Jesus prayed aloud for these fearful ones.

Christ wanted the disciples to be in the world but not of the world, to work here without belonging here. They weren't leaving as Jesus was leaving the earth. They were entering into a lions' den, a world where attendees in deadly arenas would raise or lower thumbs to decide the fate of God's chosen. So he wanted them to conduct themselves as citizens of heaven, which they were, and not to adapt again to the wrong ways of the world. So he asked God to sanctify James, Philip and Nathaniel, along with their companions.

Dietrich Bonhoeffer wrote about the cost of following Jesus faithfully, a cost the people in the upper room were beginning to learn. Bonhoeffer said, "To deny oneself is to be aware only of Christ and no more of self, to see only him who goes before and no more the road which is too hard for us. Once more, all that self-denial can say is: 'He leads the way, keep close to him.'"As he petitioned God for the disciples' sanctification, Jesus hoped they would deny themselves and follow him once again.

His prayer was for you to be sanctified, too. You're part of a long line of witnesses that stretches from Galilee to Golgotha, Jerusalem to Rome, Europe to America, the new world to all the globe, perhaps someday beyond the earth. As Jesus asked his Father, "Sanctify them," about the disciples, he included you in his request. You need to be changed, improved, made useful for the sovereign reign of God over a restored humanity. As the path to this glorious future was not easy for Jesus to walk with success, it'll be a difficult journey of frequent opposition, misunderstanding, and perhaps hatred for you. To come at last into the kingdom prepared for his people, you'll need a fortitude you don't have within you. Self-denial will be required, a self-refusal you can't make under your own ability. The repudiation of your will in favor of God's will is given by grace from him who calls you to be as holy as he is. It demands the conversion of your behavior as well as your heart. Will you allow his Spirit to improve your character so that you can be as useful as he desires? Then open the word he gave you. Let its hands massage your spiritual muscles and make you ready for service.

But this isn't quite the end of Jesus' lessons in this part of his upper room prayer. Your Lord committed himself fully to the disciples, and to you. He wanted to see them (together with you) fully committed to him. He prayed about this, too. He asked God to keep the whole church safe by making it like himself, faithfully dedicated to serve the Father by loving people, even people who refused to accept salvation, the very world that doesn't understand we who are Christians. Jesus wanted his work to continue via disciples—ancient or postmodern—you and me. Examine your commitment. Have you shouldered a cross, denied yourself and started to follow? Are you becoming whom Jesus wants you to be?

WHEN I LIVED IN METROPOLITAN BOSTON, I used to pass the Charles Street Jail on occasion. In the 1960's the jail was allowed to deteriorate and became infamous for its overcrowded, filthy cells. Pigeons messed everywhere. While I was living in the area, the jail was condemned, but prisoners were still housed in it until the 1990's. Yet a transformation occurred in the building. A developer bought it and renovated the place. Today, you can stay in a luxury room that will cost you anywhere from $300 to $5,000 per night! You can have a drink in an upscale bar called the *Alibi* or eat at a swanky restaurant called the *Clink.*

Here's a good illustration of what it means to be sanctified. Through his Son, God gets hold on your life. He brooms away the debris of your bad choices, your wrong attitudes, poor behavior—the effects of your sin— and he renovates who you are inside and outside. He makes you a clean and holy place for his Spirit to bear witness to a life made new again. Others come to him through you, because they see a renewed human soul and want to savor its richness for themselves. God markets his good news through the re-creation his grace effects in your daily behavior and your inner fruitfulness. The intensity of your new life declares for others to hear that you have been sanctified in the world, and they begin to hunger for the depth and fullness only the Christ gives.

The Lord scrutinizes what you do, where you go, what you say. He scuttles your mislaid plans and causes you to float into directions you hadn't noticed, on eddies created by his Spirit in the stream of your life. You reach horizons you never dreamed you would see. A new, eternal world is stretched out before you.

All of this comes because Jesus prays that his disciples will be sanctified in the world. However, a question remains before you: "Will I choose to live the better life the Master lays before me?"

Chapter Six

Unity for Witness

WATCHING A TELEVISION PROGRAM ABOUT FISH, I learned some interesting facts. In the ocean, herring swim in schools so plentiful you can barely distinguish individual fish. Yet they orchestrate their passage through the sea in full harmony. If they come upon an underwater barrier, the school splits in two. Half goes around the barricade one way, and the other swims on the opposite side out of sight. Yet their symphony continues without disruption. Each herring moves in concert with all the others, and the two halves of the school arrive at the opposite end of the barrier at the same time! Although separated for a time, they swim as if they respond to the baton of a single maestro. What an amazing example of unity!

Jesus continued praying for the disciples as well as the future church. He prayed that all believers would have a unified witness in the world. Though disparate people, Christ desires our unity. Consider his meaning.

In the Shadow with Jesus

The Message

The first thing to hear in this brief portion of our Lord's high priestly prayer challenges those of us who want to be sincere in following him. *Jesus prayed for all who believe the Christian message.* He looked down the long corridor that stemmed from his time on earth and saw those of us who'd take up the faith we received from his initial disciples. "My prayer is not for them alone," he told his Father. "I pray also for those who will believe in me through their message, that all of them may be one, Father, just as you are in me and I am in you. May they also be in us so that the world may believe that you have sent me" (Jn. 17:20-21). Have you listened to what he asked? Jesus asked that you and I might share the same experience he and God the Father share. Oneness. Unity. Think about what his request means.

The Lord Jesus petitioned God for the unity of Christians. Everybody who heard the apostles' message needed to be fused together as if bits of clay were added one to another and compressed into a cohesive ball, out of which an artist could sculpt a delightful figure.

The twin goals of Jesus' mission, established in heaven before the first day of creation, were the salvation of the chosen and responsive ones among earth's transgressing population, together with the erection of a church that

94

continued the process of deliverance for an indefinite amount of time between Jesus' first and second comings, an epoch set by God's private decision. How would the church fulfill its mission? By witness. Offering its unique testimony from human being to human being, the church was to tell about the achievements of Christ on the cross and in the heart. To be successful in its task, the church needed a unified witness. Jesus perceived this better than the disciples while they were in the upper room on their last night together with him. In the evening shadows and by candlelight, Jesus pressed an important thought into their beleaguered minds. He prayed for his people's unity, both those who already had faith and future people who'd yet believe. After the eleven and others after them began to speak about him, Jesus knew a church was to be born in the world.

But why must there be a witness from a church, from Christian people like you and me to people who are not yet believers in Jesus Christ? Can't humanity find its own salvation? Isn't everybody on the same quest for rescue?

Consider what Mary Emily Case said about humans who live in a world without God, a world where it's believed some natural force is sufficient to rescue you from woe. In 1892, she wrote in *The Love of the World*,

> Man is not a child of nature; he is a child of God. What is
> nature? The all-mother? Strange mother! Blind and deaf;

pitiless, or powerless to aid; who torments her children for a few brief years with meaningless and useless sufferings, then blots them out as [if] they had never been. What is nature? Matter, force, and law. Which of these shall be just? Which of them shall show mercy? Which shall help or save? Nature is not our parent. She cannot even reveal to us a parent. Nature reveals power, and not with certainty anything else. Is it an intelligent power? Is it a beneficent power? We know not. Call it, then, the unknowable, and escape despair if you can. Our case is worse than that of the ancient pagan world, inasmuch as an *unknowable* is infinitely farther off than an *unknown*. ...Knowing Christ, we know God, a father, a redeemer, a sufferer. No other but a suffering God for such a world as this. Nature and man, suffering and sin, a black, black world. But into that world light is come.

Your sincere witness, taken collectively with other Christian testimonies, is mandatory. If people whom you and I care about are to discover how truly ludicrous it is to trust in their own biological and psychological selves for answers to life's troubles, we have to express well the things Jesus accomplished. Our witness must be unified! Christ showed us the Father who loves us! the God who redeems us! Unless our friends hear the good news from you and me and others like us, they'll continue to invest the invisible powers of the creation with an exaggerated ability to deliver them from the vanity of life in a fallen environment. This is why our witness must succeed, why we must get the message of Christ into people's thoughts and discussions: *God loves you! Why not love him in return?* Here's our singular gospel, our cohesive message! This is what Jesus requested from his Father...that you and I and all his people explain his wonderful news.

He also prayed for the resemblance of Christians to himself and God. We share a family likeness with the Father and his only begotten Son. In his petition, Jesus requested "...that all of them may be one, Father, just as you are in me and I am in you." From the beginning, the Christian community was never intended to consist of independent, isolated people who go private directions, doing anything they please with no regard from one to another. The objective of heaven was that earth become part of the clan, the kith and kin of the Trinity and the angels. Our citizenship is in heaven, although we inhabit earth.

The Church is a fellowship of redeemed people who belong, not simply to God's realm, but also to one another in this realm. Just as you could never retrieve a single lump of the clay used by a sculptor to make his statue once it was completed, the church is a unit. Every believer is part of other believers, and the unity resembles the oneness of Father and Son. God and Jesus both acted in your salvation, and mine, and those other people in the pews. The Trinity continues to do this. What's more, the divine trio have never once disagreed about how our redemption should be achieved. They worked out all the details and carried out the plan they devised. Now we're expected to reflect the shining glory of their unity in who we are, what we do, where we go, and so on. Our daily lifestyle is supposed to conduct the family business with integrity, flexibility, and tender regard for those who encounter us on our appointed rounds.

While discussing the sin of gossip in his book *Getting Along With Each Other*, Richard L. Strauss raised the matter of Christian unity. "Most of us who know the Lord want our conversations to honor Him," he wrote. "We want our communication habits to promote love and unity in the Body of Christ. But too often we use our built-in weapons system to accomplish the very opposite effect. Then we wonder why there is so much conflict among God's people."

Congregations are disturbed when members of the family gossip about one another, or when we sin in other ways, but how distressing it is for non-Christians when they become privileged to information about a church's disunity and antagonisms! Potential believers fail to come to faith in our Lord, when they observe a church that isn't any better than groups of human beings outside our sacred walls.

I once lived in a community where a congregation emblazoned across a sign in front of its church building:

"The friendliest church in town!" When the congregation disintegrated over a theological issue and attendance dwindled to nearly nothing, other people in the town—many of whom were churchgoers themselves—laughed and mocked at the slogan. People asked me, "Why can't churches be truly friendly?" As a neighboring pastor, I had a lot of public relationship work to do with townsfolk over the next year.

Our Lord knew what he was praying for when he asked his Father to make the church one, to give it a like-mindedness that resembled the Trinity's oneness. As the song says, "Yes, they'll know we are Christians by our love." The unity of our shared declarations and activities as the body of Christ is crucial to the success of Jesus' sacrificial death on the cross, because we carry on the work he started. To authenticate his message requires us to demonstrate the authenticity of our message. What an awesome responsibility you and I have!

Jesus prayed for the success of Christians' unified witness. "...May they also be in us so that the world may believe that you have sent me" (Jn. 17:21b). The purpose for you and me and the rest of Christianity being like-minded and acting in concert—as the herring perform their symphony in the ocean—is that other people may believe the truth about Jesus Christ. He came to rescue our neighbors outside the church when they observe our oneness in action and witness. Jesus prayed a special prayer for all who believe the Christian message. He asked that our voices might build on the unison of a melody begun in heaven! He deeply desired that others join us in singing his song!

The Glory

The second thing to hear in this portion of Jesus' high priestly prayer is this: *He prayed for all who received his Father's glory.* "I have given them the glory that you gave me, that they may be one as we are one: I in them and you in me," he told his Father. "May they be brought to complete unity to let the world know that you sent me and have loved them even as you have loved me" (Jn. 17:22-23). You've received God's glory...what an amazing idea!

Have you listened carefully to what your Lord asked his Father? Jesus asked that you and I and other believers will share the experience he and God the Father share. *Glory! One another's shining presence!* Jesus wanted us to live in intimacy with himself, with the Father in heaven, and with each other on earth. The shining majesty of God becomes visible when the fellowship of Christians in the world discovers how to gleam together, how to sparkle for the sake of Jesus Christ and others. Glory be to God! And glory be upon his people!

You may not find this thought an easy one to accept, but since Jesus asked God to make this experience come to pass, you and I must figure out how to adapt ourselves to it without becoming either big-headed or brazen about it. We participate in the glory of God! What on earth can this mean?

Throughout the high priestly prayer of John 17, Jesus focused and refocused the disciples' attention on the idea of glory. In fact, glory is a major theme running through the entire Gospel of John. The movement of the gospel's plot line is toward Jesus' glorification. His glory is found in his death, resurrection and ascension. By dying for humanity's sins, by returning to life, and by taking up his heavenly stature and position again, Jesus Christ's glory was revealed to humanity, or at least to the portion of humanity willing to observe the events with eyes of faith.

Being brought into his glorious presence begins with a your belief. When faith operates in your heart, it shows you the truth about Christ. Not all truth is discovered by inferences drawn from detailed observations. Some facts go beyond the detection of eye, ear, or nose. They cannot be tasted with a tongue or felt with a hand. Your heart teaches you while the Holy Spirit connects dots that were speckled across life's surface by a divine artist. You see God's drawing form slowly, but the beauty of it grows. Belief is the charcoal that outlines the mysterious portrait of Jesus' glory. As with all dynamic and emotive works of art, reverence rises within your soul as you observe the picture unfold. Faith helps you understand the ways of God, his Son, and Spirit.

In *The Godhood of God*, Arthur W. Pink described a major characteristic of his era (the 1800's) as being irreverence. "By irreverence," he wrote, "I am not now thinking of open blasphemy, or the taking of God's name in vain. Irreverence is, also, failure to ascribe the glory which is due the great and dreadful majesty of the Almighty. It is the limiting of his power and actions by our degrading conceptions: it is the bringing of the Lord God *down to our level.*"

As I assess the early twenty first century, I believe such irreverence continues. Even many churchgoers look at Jesus as primarily a human being. They celebrate his humanity and confess his divinity in their creeds but not always in their hearts. We have so de-sanctified Christ that his heavenly glory eludes us. How can those of us who see mainly his humanity expect to share an example of his majesty within our own behavior? How will anyone see the glory of Christ and the Father if they see none of it in me—in my character and behavior? or in you and your conduct?

Still, Jesus prayed (in the *past tense*) for me, and you, and all who believe he's the Savior and Lord of their lives.

He declared that we already have his glory: "I *have given* them the glory that you gave me, that they may be one as we are one: I in them and you in me" (Jn. 17:22-23*a*). You and I are in possession of the Lord's glory at this moment. Wow! What does that mean?

Remember the Old Testament cloud that revealed the glorious presence of God before the marching Israelites and at the tabernacle in the wilderness as well as at the Jerusalem temple? Here's a hint about the meaning of *glory*. Also, recall the cloud at the transfiguration of Jesus. Again, a display of divine glory—God's presence with his people. We think of glory as an otherworldly light, a luminous and unearthly glow. Yet glory is mundane, an experience of this globe, this world. Glory enters into our human understanding as an awareness of God's presence with us. Jesus brings among us the attendance of the divine in our worship, the company of the Almighty in our crisis, the presence of our Father to comfort. Jesus is with us; God is with us. Jesus is Immanuel! He's glorious!

When you and I undertake the behavioral lifestyle of Jesus Christ, along with his psychological disposition, we take up his glory, his presence as a life-breathing reality. The Holy Spirit is the presence of God within you, and as you follow his lead in acts of mercy, kindness, generosity, peace and holiness, you yourself become an embodiment of heaven on earth. You're God's presence with a sufferer or a doubter just as Jesus was his presence with you. Each Christian participates in the glory of Father and Son. And other people notice it! That's why some who are afraid of God shun you, and why other people who want to know him come to you as a friend or a seeker. They sense the glory of Christ remolding your character. Neither you nor they would probably explain the attraction in this way, but the words you choose to describe it do not change the experience you're describing. You've been given the glory of God by the Son of God so that you may reflect him accurately in the world while you walk through it in his name. You didn't create the glory within you, and you have no right or privilege to claim it as a possession. Nevertheless, the glory is in you, and it's visible in who you are, what you do, where you go, what you say. Those to whom you're sent see it, and on the basis of what they see they respond with animosity or friendship. The response is in proportion to their willingness to doubt or to believe God has truly brought you into his family.

The Lord Jesus prayed that all Christians should reproduce the Father and Son's unity. You and I and the other members of our congregations are supposed to be a single body of believers. We're to work together, seeking the guidance of the Holy Spirit. He'll show us what to do, where to go, what to say, who to be as we work at being God's people. Whenever we combine our lives and efforts into a synchronized witness to the people around us, we display on earth the agreeable concord of heaven. The unity we display also exhibits our Master's glory. Those to whom he sends us cannot help but notice it. Some are attracted to it, while others are repelled by it. Our job is to show the Lord's glory in our characters. He achieves what he wishes, and we have only cause for humility. It's his glory we reflect.

Jesus prayed that Christians would proclaim the message of the gospel. He was finished with the core teaching about how to please God. Now he entrusted the message to eleven disciples who hadn't betrayed him. Later he included the apostle Paul and countless other believers in the church's first generation as bearers of his glory. Across twenty centuries and now into another one, the gospel has passed from generation to generation, age to age, by moving from person to person, you to someone else. Jesus prayed that you'd tell others about him and about the possibilities he created for human betterment. "May they be brought to complete unity to let the world know that you sent me and have loved them even as you have loved me" (Jn. 17:23).

In other words, Jesus prayed that you succeed in your witness. As you speak what he teaches you across the decades of your life, you have a positive effect. You may not see much interest as you tell people what good Jesus does for you and them, but he himself asked God to bring your words to good ends. He asked the Father to ensure that your good deeds, done in his name and by his Spirit's leading, will succeed in God's objective. So forget what circumstances seem to say. Do Christ's will, because he guarantees you cannot fail! Especially when you act in concert with other believers!

I DON'T KNOW if it still stands, but a traveler described a tree he saw in New Jersey. In a field where the trees had been cut down and made into charcoal, one remaining tree stood twenty-five yards from the highway. It was so strange a sight the traveler stopped to study it. About eight or ten feet from each other two trunks rose upward, but five or six feet overhead, they angled toward each other. Then they joined into a single trunk. The tree continued to grow skyward, but now it had only one treetop. Another wonderful example of Christian unity!

In the upper room, near the end of his final evening with the disciples, Jesus prayed that all believers will have a unified witness in the world, one that will display his glory to anyone who cares to see it.

How well are you helping the heavenly Father answer your Savior's prayer?

Chapter Seven

Before Creation and Now

CAN YOU SUMMARIZE JESUS' LIFE AND WITNESS? He himself recapitulated it as he prayed for all believers. Study what he said. What were the truths behind his service? God's presence and love were his two great lessons. Have you learned these principles?

Jesus' high priestly prayer was almost ended. He'd soon lead his people to Gethsemane to continue praying, but they'd fall asleep. It's good he encapsulated his witness in the upper room, or it might have been missed entirely. His closing words condensed what he said during the years the disciples walked Palestine's roads with him, but they were full of food, drowsy, and missed his words' importance.

Knowing His Presence

Jesus prayed that all believers will know his presence. "Father," he said, "I want those you have given me to be with me where I am, and to see my glory, the glory you have given me because you loved me before the creation of the world" (Jn. 17:24). The major focus of his request was on the future, not our time, but a time yet to come. He meant the day when human salvation would be completed. He asked the Father to bring all his people to heaven, to show them the glory and love he and the Father shared before the creation. He kept his orientation on the eternal. He looked back to his association with the Father before anything was made; then he looked toward a distant future when all he started was perfected.

You and I need an eternal perspective, yet it's difficult for us to maintain the outlook for long. Memories of the few times when our minds or hearts pierce the shadows of time and see the everlasting dimensions of God's realm keep us interested, intrigued by all that might last forever. Soon we lose the prospect. We slip back into the confines of a clock and calendar. We're meant for eternity. God has hidden it in our hearts, but we're bound by the limitations of our days and souls. By God's design, we who have faith in Christ are destined to share eternity with the Lord.

Jesus prayed that we'd be with him and see his glory. Allow the excitement of the Son's petition to the Father to settle over you. Isn't it wonderful to know you'll be with Christ in the future? You'll see the eternal glory he received because the Father loved him prior to loving you, me, and all of creation. What love and glory it must be!

H. C. G. Moule, teaching on the high priestly prayer, wrote about the idea of eternal life with Christ: "To be with him, to be so with him as to see him, so to see him as to behold his glory, given him by his Father—this is enough, and only this could be enough, to make tangible, credible, infinitely desirable, the hope of an endless heaven"

The blissful future that awaits Christians is delightful to contemplate only because it centers on the Father's Son. Any other motive for entering the eternal realm would be selfishness, and aren't the hopes of so many for "being saved and going to heaven" really a thinly veiled self-interest? Make knowing and loving Jesus in heaven as you've known and loved him on earth the goal for your desire to be with him for eternity. The peace and pleasure of God's home will be your possession both then and now. As Moule suggested, concentrate on anything except Jesus and being in heaven will become boring in time.

Entrance into the heavenly glory is a matter of grace, just as salvation itself is dependent on mercy. God gave Jesus a people from the world. First, the disciples. Then, all who believed in him because of their witness, and because of the witness of later Christians like you and me. We've received a dynamic relationship with the Father, Son, and

109

the Spirit. As we witness to our good experience with the Trinity, other folks can discover the love and glory of God for themselves. Jesus asked the Father to bring every one of the redeemed into the heavenly realm so they might be rewarded by observing the fellowship of the Trinity and the church. They'd see Christ's glory, his presence. He knew that the future was safely in God's hands alone, and how entering heaven is a divine gift.

How do you and I and others perceive God's glory in his Son? How is the Spirit related to our discernment? John Wesley expressed it well when he wrote, "Tell me how it is that in this room there are three candles and but one light, and I will explain to you the mode of divine existence." Jesus prayed that you and I, together with the original disciples, as well as all believers across time, would know the glory of the love held for him in heaven. From the cross to the consummation of the eternal kingdom, Christians learn a truth they barely experience but truly understand. "Jesus loves me!" So I will praise his glory now! And then I shall see him face to face!

This is a promise to you and me in Jesus' prayer. The older I get, the more trials I've seen, the more this promise of coming into God's presence and seeing Christ's majesty means to me. Do you believe it'll happen for you? I pray the Father's love for Christ will be visible to you more every day. It will also teach you to trust his love for you. Such a knowledge sustains a weary soul!

Now, think about what Jesus wanted. He desired his people to be with him. Earlier that evening in the upper room, he told those around the table: "In my Father's house are many rooms; if it were not so, I would have told you. I am going there to prepare a place for you. And if I go and prepare a place for you, I will come back and take you to be with me that you also may be where I am" (Jn. 14:2-3). At Christian funerals, pastors often read this statement as a reminder to mourners that their believing loved ones are in God's presence. You have both Jesus' promise and prayer from the upper room. Grip them tightly! He wants you to be with him. Wow! What a thought! Do you feel the marvel in it? Make the promise a still point, a firm rock, in your faith. Knowing you're destined to stand before God and to live with him forever will keep your behavior in check and your heart strong as you go into the valleys of life.

Jesus also wanted his people to see his glory. As we've heard before, the bright cloud that enveloped Jesus at the transfiguration, and a cloud that brightened the Jerusalem temple when it was dedicated, and the pillar of cloud that guided the Israelites in their desert wandering, were the indications of God's presence, his glory. In heaven, you'll see the eternal brightness—the glory—of Christ Jesus. It's a magnificence and beauty he possessed before the earth was formed, before the universe existed or ever the sun rose. Jesus owned the grandeur because the Father loved him. In relationship with the Father, the Son found his splendor. You see, laurels and triumph, success and fame, don't come because of your achievements. Glory comes because you're loved. Jesus was loved from all eternity. Everything admirable and praiseworthy in him was due to a relationship with his Father. This is what he wanted his people to see about him, and about themselves.

How I wish we could all keep this thought clearly! But you and I, and so many employees, politicians, business people, authors, and actors think stardom comes because of our talents, honed and sharpened into tools we use to make people praise us. Our glory is temporary in this world, because we seek to create it ourselves. Truth is, our glory—our reputation, our triumphs—can't endure unless it grows out of love's soil. Your glory isn't attached to what you do, but to whom you love and who loves you.

The wife of someone I know talks about her husband's sister. She's much younger than her brother, and every time the two siblings are together, the sister hangs on every word the brother says and marvels at all he accomplishes. He's glorious in her eyes! Why? It isn't what he does that creates her admiration. His sister's love for him gives him an attractive brilliance. Love always precedes glory. You can do nothing to make your name last forever without the love of those who will remember you fondly.

So it has always been with Jesus Christ. His glory is rooted in the Father's love! A love Jesus knew before day one of creation. This is why he prayed for all Christians to enter heaven after the work of salvation is completed. He wants you and me to see the love that flows between God and himself. Then we'll truly appreciate his magnificence, because we'll share in their love. Until you see the love of God for his only begotten Son, you won't grasp the significance of heaven, nor will you be grateful for the eternal kingdom, nor will you welcome the rule of the Sovereign God over all aspects of your life, nor will you know all that it means to be loved by God yourself.

In the beauty of a relationship with Christ lies the glory of your own character and the ground for your admission through the Pearly Gates. The more perfectly you come to love Christ, the more clearly you triumph as a person, the more honestly people love and praise you. Discover how to love the Lord without any reservation, or heaven will be a disinteresting place. The misconception about heaven will evaporate if you love Jesus. Believe me when I say that sitting on a cloud, strumming a harp won't cut it for more than a day or two. Unless you eagerly long to be in the presence of him who loves you, heaven is a non-enchanted realm. And be honest. Although human beings you love may be in heaven waiting for you, don't you recall reasons why you might not want to see them again? Without an abiding fellowship with Jesus Christ, heaven may only be a repeat of earth's hard times. The glory of heaven is found when you know the love of heaven.

All of this was the personal experience of the man called Jesus of Nazareth as he prayed in his Father's presence, and he understood how it'll be your experience, too.

Thinking along these lines, I discover that Jesus' prayer applies not only to the future, but it applies to today as well. Earlier that evening, he explained the Holy Spirit's work during the earthly lives of all Christian people. The Spirit, he said, "...will bring glory to me by taking from what is mine and making it known to you" (Jn. 16:14). Jesus' prayer is to be fulfilled grandly when you join him in heaven, but even now you and I discover his glory when his Spirit, who lives within each of us who believe, teaches us what Jesus himself taught. In other words, as you learn to love your neighbor as you love yourself, you find God's glory—his presence within you and in the Christian people around you. In your relationships with other believers, you become like Christ and the Father. The love you hold for a friend at church brings you a desire to be helpful to him or her. You want to listen to the person's woes and joys, and you console or rejoice as the need reveals itself. Because you care for the other believer, your friend looks to you with respect and honors your name, your person. You're credited with the beauty of a kind and generous person. Though you shun the praise, it finds you out. Others see you as a respectable church member, an example of the grace of God active in human life. They learn from who you are and what you do how to live successfully by the principles of Jesus Christ. Your witness for him is bright and glowing, not so much because of deeds you do as because of the love Jesus is able to express through you. While you grow in Christian demeanor, while you become like your Savior, others praise you for what he improves in you. It's impossible for you to claim such glory. It is given out of God's love that flows through you to others. And that's more valuable than any laurels society may lay on your head, isn't it? So seek the presence of Christ in yourself and in those around you, and you'll be surprised at the wonder he brings into your days and the humility he puts in your heart.

Knowing His Love

Jesus also prayed that all believers will know his love. "Righteous Father," he said, "though the world does not know you, I know you, and they know that you have sent me. I have made you known to them, and will continue to make you known in order that the love you have for me may be in them and that I myself may be in them" (Jn. 17:25-26). The people whom God did not give to Jesus— people who disbelieve—don't know God. They think they know him, but either they understand him vaguely or they pick up a substitute god. Jesus said his followers know that the Father sent him. He revealed God to his people, and through the disciples' faithful witness, others would come to believe in Christ. During his earthly ministry, Jesus disclosed the Father, and he continues to do so now. Why? So that his people experience the love which the eternal Son and Father have had for one another since before the universe was created. The Lord wanted his people to have fellowship with one another and with himself and the heavenly Father. Wow! This is pretty heady stuff!

It sounds like repetition of what we've been discussing. However, as we continue filtering through the closing words of Jesus' high priestly prayer, we're led into deeper levels of life with him. So let's press on.

Think about Jesus' promise. He wanted his people to continue knowing God the Father. The disciples must experience life with God, along with the hope and vitality he brings to human days, not to mention the help he sends in their times of trouble. You and I need this experience, and Jesus prayed that we, as well as the original disciples, would have it. He wanted you to continue understanding God, to have a living relationship with him.

Do you know God loves you? I mean, are there feelings of comfort and enjoyment in your heart as you think about the Almighty? Does he help you in every circumstance? When you're pushed by somebody to do what you sense might be a bit shady, are you aware of divine assistance as you resist the temptation? Then you're experiencing the answer to Jesus' prayer. The Father is with you. He's alive and active in your soul. He undergirds your activities as you go about your days, bringing out of your faithfulness more good than you might observe or think you achieve.

Whoa! Think about this again. God cares enough about you to be part of your daily living. It doesn't matter how you feel about it. All that matters is that you believe it happens, because this is what occurs in your Christian life all the time. You participate in the Father's answer to his Son's prayer. Praise the Lord! He *wants* to relate to you. He *does* relate to you. Hallelujah! You're never alone!

A Welsh saying goes like this: "There are three things that only God knows—the beginning of things, the cause of things, and the end of things." My experience with God tells me this is true. I'm an active person, moving about the scenery of my life. Most of the time I don't think much about God's presence and love. I take him for granted. My faith tells me I don't have to worry about whether he looks after my well-being. God is faithful, and he's never at a distance. Although a song says he's distant, the song's wrong; God is always *with* me. I don't deserve his presence, but Jesus taught me God loves me as he loved him. So I believe and trust. As I finish a day's activities, whether I've written a sermon, visited a shut-in, gone to a hospital, attended a meeting, or talked with my wife—whatever I've done—I know the Father accompanied me. I believe he used me to do more good than I know.

Over the years, I've been blessed by people who told me that something I said or did helped or comforted them. Most the time, I never thought I did something special. I just related to the people I encountered as just another person who happens to be aware of divine blessing in his life and who wants to reassure others that God is indeed beside, behind and beneath them as they walk the planet or wait for the final breath to come. In all of this, I've known—without always being aware of it—that I'm participating in the Father's answer to his Son's prayer. "I have made you known to them, and will continue to make you known in order that the love you have for me may be in them and that I myself may be in them" (Jn. 17:26).

I don't often perceive the beginning, the cause, or the end of things, but I can think of no higher adventure than living this kind of life with my Lord. He amazes me all the time, because he knows where I've come from, why, and where I'm going. So I praise him for using me to show his love to a world that seldom notices it. I pray that you do, or will, experience the same exciting activity in your day-to-day living. Such a faith journey deeply satisfies the soul.

Think more about Jesus' promise in his high priestly prayer's closing words. He wanted his people to continue knowing his own love, not just the Father's love. When his followers came to understand God's love for Jesus himself, they'd understand Christ's love for them as well.

Paul wrote about love: "It always protects, always trusts, always hopes, always perseveres" (1 Cor. 13:7). But answers to life's woes—which is why love must protect, trust, hope and persevere—weren't the only concern in Jesus' mind. Approaching his cross, he understood he was dying so that sin could be removed from human beings, but he also perceived another mundane need his death would answer: the experience of people who learn about his tenderness, devotion and passion for them. His love may comfort you in your anguish, but isn't it also a joy in your happiest days? Don't you sense the closeness and support of Christ's hand when life is hard? Don't you sense the same hand raised in excitement when you're delighted by the fellowship you have with him and his church? Then you're experiencing in *your* life the answer to Jesus' prayer. You're coming closer to him. You relate to both the living God and the living Savior. Wow! Jesus wasn't merely a man who showed people how to touch the Creator of the universe. He was a person who loved other people and touched them himself.

Christ prayed that you'd learn of heaven's love so that he himself—Jesus!—could enter into you. Think about this. Jesus *in* you. What does the word *in* mean? We pass over it so frequently and fail to consider its significance. We assume we know what the two letters say. Yet what's the word *in* mean? The first things that come to mind are *inside, within, into*. Jesus arrives inside you. He's within you. He enters into your experience. But there's more! The word *in* also carries the idea of *during*, as in the phrase *in the 1960's* means *during the 1960's*. Jesus is in your life; he relates to you during your lifetime. Christ flows into your hours and days, weeks and years. His feeling for you causes him to take up your company throughout every activity. Rejoice in the Lord! He never leaves nor forsakes you, since he lives in you! As the hymn declares, "You ask me how I know he lives? He lives within my heart."

The love of Jesus surrounds and fills you. It matters nothing that you may not feel him inside you. He's there, expanding into your heart and mind. He takes a share in all you do. Jesus participates in your daily affairs. He makes himself a major feature of your personality. It's as if you wear him like a sweater beneath your winter coat. Paul was getting at this idea when he wrote,

> You were taught, with regard to your former way of life, to put off your old self, which is being corrupted by its deceitful desires; to be made new in the attitude of your minds; and to put on the new self, created to be like God in true righteousness and holiness.
>
> Ephesians 4:22-24

To have Jesus Christ in your life means you're taking on a holy and divine life. You don't become a deity, a god, but you receive God's Son into your person. Through his Holy Spirit, Jesus resides in your emotions and mind. You undergo his feelings for others and ponder his thoughts about people and their behavior, as well as your conduct toward them. With Jesus in you, a transformation starts to occur. Holiness grows. You become Christlike.

Meditate on this! You become like the Nazarene in your rational powers. You stop considering the trinkets and pastimes of fallen humanity to be of first importance. Believe it or not, this happened: A sinful husband allowed his sick wife to moan in bed with no caring attention while he watched a football game in the family room. Not only that, but the family's two children had the flu and were in bed, too! What a horrible family dynamic was played out in this non-believer's home! However, a Christian husband and father who has Jesus alive within him could not do such an atrocious deed. A televised football game can be enjoyed, but not if it makes you neglect any ailing person in your home. Relationships with people around you become paramount when Jesus takes up residence in your soul. As the apostle John said, "We love because he first loved us" (1 Jn. 4:19). Your ability to reason and to love become equivalent to the thoughtful reflection and the caring compassion Jesus expresses for people.

MEDITATE DEEPLY ON JESUS' WORDS to the heavenly Father: "I have made you known to them, and will continue to make you known in order that the love you have for me may be in them and that I myself may be in them" (Jn. 17:26). This was God's intention for his Son, Jesus of Nazareth, before the universe was created. It remains his intention now for you, his redeemed child.

Made in the USA
Middletown, DE
12 May 2023

30418721R00076